THE SUCCULENTS DESIGN BOOK

Container Combinations that Look Great and Thrive Together Year-Round

Kentaro
Kuroda

TUTTLE Publishing

Tokyo | Rutland, Vermont | Singapore

Contents

Why I Wrote This Book

By casually creating succulent arrangements and seeing each individual plant, I make new discoveries and feel energized and encouraged every day.

Moved by flower buds that come up from between the nodes, I smile at the sight of strangely-shaped leaves that change color with the changing seasons. I marvel when I discover slight changes in pots in which I'm cultivating cuttings, and I feel relieved when I manage to create a good arrangement.

In this book, I've packed lots of tips I've learned from my many mistakes to help you enjoy creating your own arrangements. I explain the process in as much detail as possible—everything from choosing seedlings and pots to managing your arrangement after creation.

The recipes for each of the twelve months of the year use seedlings you can find at gardening stores and online. From small, easy arrangements to large and varied container gardens, I take you step-by-step with detailed instructions and illustrations. I hope this content will help you fully enjoy creating you own succulent container gardens. Once you get the hang of how to plant and care for succulents, you'll find that arrangements are easy to make, and are hardier and easier to manage than you might think. You'll be overwhelmed by the variety and depth of charm that unique succulents have to offer. That is why they're so much fun to arrange and grow!

No matter how matter how I try to explain it, the actual creation of a container garden and the excitement you feel from completing it can't be described. I would like to give everyone a chance to enjoy that feeling.

Succulents are beautiful, funny, and interesting plants that you never get tired of looking at. That makes the challenge of arranging them among the most pleasant and satisfying things you'll ever experience.

— **Kentaro Kuroda**

Notes about this book

■ Generally, the focus throughout this book is on potted succulents and seedlings that are commonly available at gardening stores.

■ This book utilizes scientific names, as these are the plants' universal identifiers. Most of the plants used here can be found in most parts of the world. We describe the characteristics and features of each plant used in this book on pages 143–147. Basic advice on how to grow and use the plants in groupings can also be found at the back of the book.

■ **In the instructions, plants will be referred to by their species/variety/hybrid names.**

■ The data in this book is based on the climate around Tokyo, which has a hardiness zone of 30–35°F (-1.1–1.7°C) and tends to be least humid in January and most humid in July. Be sure to check the hardiness zone for your region and make cultivation management decisions based on temperature and humidity highs and lows.

JANUARY

Vibrant Variations in Midwinter Colors

In winter, succulents that have been exposed to cold weather turn red and and other bright shades. With this arrangement I'll introduce some of the reds, pinks and oranges of winter.

A. Use Bright Red to Create a Feminine Look

Beautiful brightly-colored succulents

Many succulents turn red in late fall and winter. Unlike other plants, succulents don't shed their leaves even in winter, so you can enjoy their gorgeous colors until the cold eases up, generally around March. Also, summer-grown varieties stop growing during the dormant season, allowing the plant to keep its shape until spring. To maintain its beautiful red foliage, it needs plenty of sunlight.

During the winter, keep the plant in a dry place where the temperature does not fall below 41°F (5°C) at night. When moving outside in late April, or whenever in your region the danger of cold has passed, the foliage will gradually change to the fresh color characteristic of the growing season.

This shallow-pot stars the plant Japan calls the Himatsuri (Fire Festival), which has the most brilliantly red leaves of all winter succulents. This piece is inspired by Japanese winter and evokes a sense of harmony.

Main plant: Cassula capitella 'Campfire'
Supporting plant: Sedum pachyphyllum

Characteristics of Succulents in Winter

In winter, the garden stores carry succulents displaying beautiful leaf colors. Those placed in areas without heating have particularly vivid foliage. During this season, cold-resistant varieties dominate a store's stock, while cold-sensitive succulents like *Adenium*, *Pachypodium*, and succulents from the *Araceae* and *Euphorbiaceae* families are less widely available.

The plants are intentionally
spaced apart so that each
stands out and their leaves are
clearly visible. The bright red *Cassula
capitella* 'Campfire' planted in the foreground
catches the eye, while in the center, the *Sedum
pachyphyllum* with its subtly-colored, rounded
leaf tips is placed to create an elegant effect.

In fall, the leaves of 'Harry Butterfield' turn from pastel green to cream. 'Yellow Humbert' and 'Frosty' have a hint of red at the leaf tips, while 'Copper Spoons' turns a deep brown color.

B. Ensembles with Winter Coloring

Maintain a balance between the left and right sides while preserving the sense of movement in the foliage

Antique scales with rampant-stemmed succulents. On the right is a silver *Echeveria pulvinata* 'Frosty' with *Kalanchoe orgyalis* 'Copper Spoons', and on the left is a cream-colored *Sedeveria* 'Harry Butterfield' with reddish 'Yellow Humbert'. Both the left and right sides have a combination of bright, stylish foliage colors for contrast. In winter, mist the soil just enough to moisten the surface every 2-3 weeks, and gradually increase watering from around March.

Main plant: Sedeveria 'Harry Butterfield', Echeveria pulvinata 'Frosty'
Supporting plant: Sedeveria 'Yellow Humbert', Kalanchoe orgyalis 'Copper Spoons'

Use seedlings that can be divided to create a dense, rounded shape

Using seedlings that can be divided, we create a rounded and lush arrangement that flows from deep red to pink. Only five seedlings are used, but the color variety and spacing of the seedlings results in a rich display. Keep the plants indoors in a brightly lit window, or in cold regions, place them in the center of the room at night and early morning to maintain a minimum temperature of 41°F (5°C) or higher.

Main plant: Graptosedum 'Francesco Baldi'
Supporting plant: Sinocrassula indica

During the day, place it in a window that receives full sun. In spring, when growth starts, prune it back into shape if it becomes untidy.

JANUARY | A. Use Bright Red to Create a Feminine Look

Materials for this group planting

Layout

Plants

a. Crassula fusca

b. Crassula capitella 'Campfire'
★ Alternate = Crassula capitella

c. Aeonium decorum 'Variegata'

d. Sedum pachyphyllum
(Jelly Bean Plant)
★ Alternate = Koigokoro

e. Echeveria 'Peach Pride'

f. Echeveria harmsii

g. Adromishus hemisphaericus

Pot

Shallow bowl:
Diameter 8.25" (210mm) x Height 3.25" (80mm)
Culture soil for succulents / Root rot inhibitor

How to Plant

1 Flatten the soil and plant 'Peach Pride' in the back left corner. Ensure that the seedlings are planted straight and do not tilt.

2 Plant the 'Variegata' in front of 1, aligning its height with 1.

3 Plant the 'Campfire' in the front-right of the bowl.

4 In the space visible between the 'Campfire' and the 'Variegata' from the front view, plant the Pachyphyllum.

5 Plant Harmsii next to 4. The taller stems should face inward and the shorter stems should face outward.

6 Plant Brosplakkies behind the Harmsii.

7 Plant Fusca between 'Peach Pride' and Brosplakkies.

Tip 1: Low-height seedlings are chosen to match the container.

Since the vessel is short, we used smaller seedlings, avoiding plants with strong roots and tall stems. But if everything is planted at the same height, the arrangement will look flat and uninteresting, so use taller seedlings in the center and shorter ones around the periphery to create a gently curved silhouette.

Finished

Tip 2: Create a gorgeous feeling with the contrast of red and green.

In this grouping, the center is planted slightly higher, but the seedlings are of similar height throughout. To avoid a monotonous look, the red-leafed Fusci, 'Campfire', and Harmsii are contrasted with Peach Pride, 'Pachyphyllum', and Brosplakkies to create a crisp and lively group planting.

Materials for this group planting

Layout

Plants

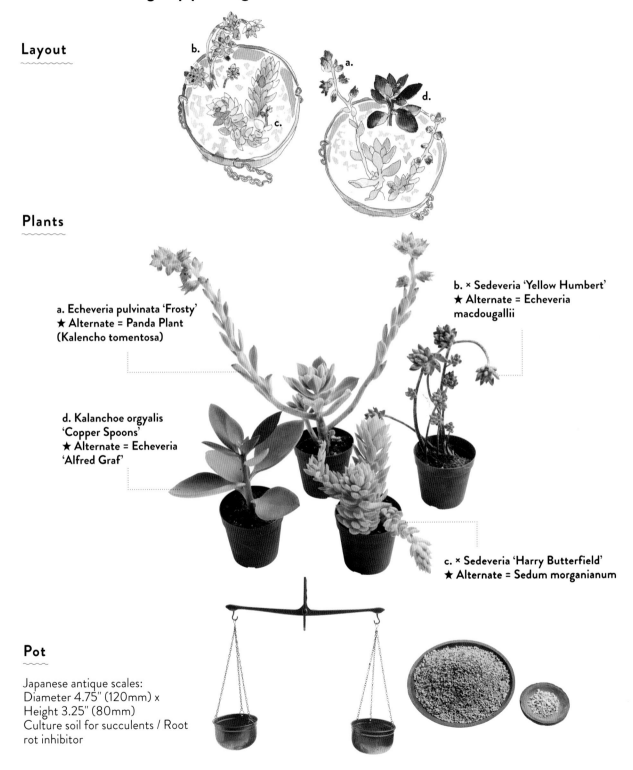

a. Echeveria pulvinata 'Frosty'
★ Alternate = Panda Plant
(Kalencho tomentosa)

b. × Sedeveria 'Yellow Humbert'
★ Alternate = Echeveria
macdougallii

d. Kalanchoe orgyalis
'Copper Spoons'
★ Alternate = Echeveria
'Alfred Graf'

c. × Sedeveria 'Harry Butterfield'
★ Alternate = Sedum morganianum

Pot

Japanese antique scales:
Diameter 4.75" (120mm) x
Height 3.25" (80mm)
Culture soil for succulents / Root
rot inhibitor

How to Plant

1 Add enough soil to cover the bottom of the container, then add a little root rot inhibitor.

2 Plant the 'Harry Butterfield' in front of the bowl on the left. The stems should flow from left to right.

3 Plant 'Yellow Humbert' in the back right corner of the container, with the stems flowing from left to right as in 2.

4 Plant 'Frosty' at the front left of the right pot.

5 Plant 'Copper Spoons' at the top right of the pot.

Finished

Tip 1: Using succulent plant culture soil as a make-up base.

This group plant uses a culture medium blended for succulents and cacti. Culture medium for succulents is made with an emphasis on drainage to prevent root damage. Because of its whitish, decorative stone-like appearance, it is recommended for modern-looking pieces or for indoor placement.

Tip 2: Decide precisely on the placement before planting!

The planting process is easy with two seedlings each, but since the left and right vessels are far apart, the key is to create a good balance between the balance and the form of the seedlings. Seedlings with moving stems should be selected, and long flower ears and stems should be directed toward the center where there is an open space. The result is a sense of unity and a cohesive mosaic.

JANUARY | C. Gothic Style with a Gradation of Colors

Materials for this group planting

Layout

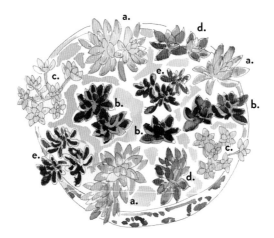

Plants

b. Graptopetalum 'Bronze'

c. Graptopetalum mendozae

a. × Graptosedum
'Francesco Baldi'
★ Alternate = Pachyphytum
oviferum (Moonstones)

e. Sedum rubrotinctum
f. variegata

d. Sinocrassula indica
★ Alternate = Crassula capitella
'Campfire'

Pot

Patterned ceramic bowl:
Diameter 6.1" (155mm) x Height 5.7" (145mm)

How to Plant

1 Divide the Mendozae and plant one in the left back corner, leaning it outward.

2 Divide the 'Francesco Baldi' into three and plant a segment next to 1. Slightly tilt it to create a semi-spherical shape.

3 Divide the 'Bronze' into three and plant a segment in front of 'Francesco Baldi', tilting it slightly outward.

4 Divide Rubrotinctum into two and plant a segment in front of 3. Tilt them outward as per the Mendozae in step 1.

5 Plant 'Francesco Baldi' in front of the left side of the pot. Tilt it outward like in step 1 and raise the central side.

6 Divide the Indica in two and plant a segment to the right front of 5, tilting it outward.

7 Plant 'Bronze' at the back right of 5. Tilt the plants slightly forward and adjust its height to match 'Francesco Baldi'.

8 Plant the remaining Mendozae at the right front of the pot. Tilt it outward to create a rounded silhouette.

9 Plant the remaining 'Bronze' and at the back of 8.

10 Plant the remaining 'Francesco Baldi' along the edge of the pot at the back right.

11 Finish by planting the rest of the divided Indica along the edge at the back of the pot.

Finished

FEBRUARY

Enjoy Poetic Combinations by a Winter Window

February is the coldest month of the year. Let's warm it up with a gorgeous collection of succulents. Colorful succulents bring beauty to a winter window and add a touch of brilliance to the surroundings.

A. Using Color with an Eye Toward Elegance

Beautifully-colored succulents that I love beside my window

Beautifully-colored succulents can transform a window. Even in the heart of winter when flowers and greenery become scarce, these succulent plants retain their beauty without shedding leaves. Some varieties, like the European-origin Sempervivum and similar plants like Manfreda, are cold-resistant, but most succulents can withstand temperatures of around 41°F (5°C).

At this time of year, it's best to keep your plants indoors. Place them near a sunny window and keep them away from the window at night when the temperature drops. If the outside temperature does not fall below 32°F (0°C), the plant can be kept under the eaves of the roof or on a balcony if you keep it slightly dry by reducing watering.

This grouping set in a brass balance scale coordinates succulents that turn red and pink in the cold weather. From deep red to a gentle pink shade in the *Graptopetalum* this work of art offers a beautiful gradation of colors.

Main plant: Echeveria 'Minibelle'
Supporting plant: Sedum prolifera

The deep foliage color creates a stately atmosphere to match antique vessels. *Sedum prolifera*, *Sedum spurium* 'Tricolor', *Scenecio herreanus*, and *Graptopetalum paraguayense* have stems that droop as they grow, naturally blending in with hanging vessels.

B. Plant Them Like Overflowing Flowers in Bloom

The differing heights and contrasting colors create a lively atmosphere

By mixing tall, medium, and low-growing plants and combining red, green (yellow), and blue-hued leaf colors that intensify in the cold, you create a visually appealing and colorful potted arrangement. For iron-made planters, as the roots are susceptible to cold, water sparingly during winter, misting them once every 2-3 weeks. Keep them slightly dry to maintain the ideal conditions.

Main plant: Echeveria 'Kakurei', Echeveria 'Queen Red'
Supporting plant: Aeonium undulatum,
Sedum adolphi (Golden glow)

Be careful with watering in winter, as the material of the pot you use can affect the soil's temperature. In spring, when the plants begin to grow, prune off overgrown stems to maintain the group's shape.

18

C. Simple Style with a Scandinavian Feel

Matching pots are displayed side by side to emphasize the individuality of each grouping

Create a lively and vibrant indoor interior by contrasting height and color in a pair of stylish matching pots. In one pot, plant succulents with round leaves; in the other, incorporate varieties with elongated or upward-growing leaves, allowing you to enjoy the delightful contrast between the two. During winter, place them in a well-lit area indoors and rotate the pots 180 degrees every 2-3 days to ensure even sunlight exposure for all the planted seedlings.

Main plant: Kalanchoe millotii (right), Senecio antandroi (left)
Supporting plant: Crassula atropurpurea var. Watermeyeri (right), Crassula 'jade Necklace' (left)

These plants do best in rooms that aren't heated extensively. Even in a heated room, the beautiful foliage colors can be enjoyed near a window where the temperature drops at night. In winter, water once every 2-3 weeks in the morning with a mist sprayer. Ensure that the soil dries out slightly by evening.

FEBRUARY | A. Using Color with an Eye Toward Elegance

Materials for this group planting

Layout

Plants

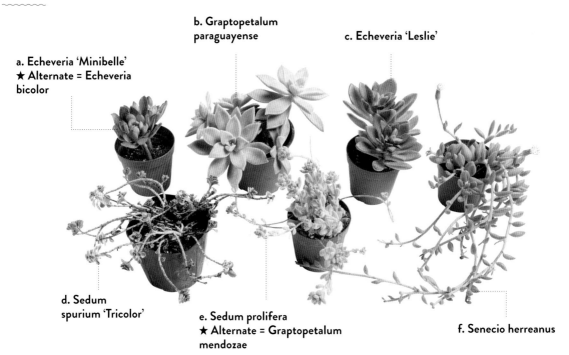

a. Echeveria 'Minibelle'
★ Alternate = Echeveria bicolor

b. Graptopetalum paraguayense

c. Echeveria 'Leslie'

d. Sedum spurium 'Tricolor'

e. Sedum prolifera
★ Alternate = Graptopetalum mendozae

f. Senecio herreanus

Pot

Antique brass scale:
Diameter 6.25" (160mm) x Height 2.75" (70mm)
Root rot inhibitor

How to Plant

1 Place potting soil mixed with some root rot inhibitor in the container, filling it to about 80 percent capacity.

2 Place the Prolifera in the center left, allowing it to overlap the handle for a natural look.

3 Plant 'Tricolor' in the front. Let the stems cascade outside the container.

4 Plant 'Minibelle' behind 3. Tilt it forward so that the rosette shapes are clearly visible.

5 Plant 'Leslie' in the right front. Tilt the plant to the edge and let it overhang the rim.

6 Plant Herreanus at the back of 5. Let the stems cascade outside the pot, directing the flow slightly forward.

7 Plant the Paraguayense in the empty space at the back. Tilt the plant slightly toward the edge and allow it to protrude outside the container.

Finished

Tip 1: Utilize the drooping stems to enhance the container's form.

The container we used is an old French balancing scale. When using a hanging display container, it's best to choose varieties with drooping stems that complement the container's shape. Here we planted Scenecio herreanus, which has lush green stems and leaves, to emphasize the contrast in shape and color with 'Minibelle' and 'Leslie'.

Tip 2: Create a sense of volume by using medium-size plants in the middle.

When planting seedlings on the edge of a container, tilt them outward so that their leaves and stems protrude from the container. This will add volume and give the arrangement a lively appearance. Plant the central seedlings perpendicular to the soil to create a plump, rounded overall shape.

FEBRUARY | B. Plant Them Like Overflowing Flowers in Bloom

Materials for this group planting

Layout

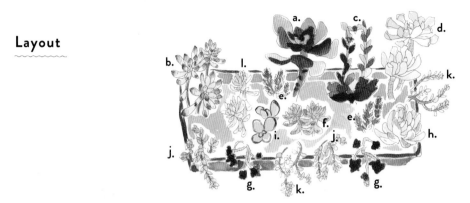

Plants

a. Echeveria 'Kakurei'

b. Echeveria macdougalii

c. Echeveria 'Queen Red'
★ Alternate = Echeveria 'Opalaina'

d. Aeonium undulatum
★ Alternate = Echeveria pallida

e. Villadia batesii

f. Sedum adolphi 'Golden Glow'
★ Alternate = Sedum 'Sunrise Mom'

g. Sedum spurium 'Dragon's Blood'

h. × Pachyveria 'Scheideckeri'

i. Kalanchoe scapigera

j. Crassula remota

k. Sedum album 'Athorum'

l. × Sedeveria 'Yellow Humbert'

Pot

Steel horizontal planter:
Width 23.75" (600mm) x Depth 2.75" (70mm) x Height 3.5" (90mm)

How to Plant

1. Plant the Macdougalii on the left, placing it toward the back and tilting it to the front left.

2. Divide the Remota into two segments and plant them in the front left, letting the stems hang over the edge of the pot.

3. Place the 'Yellow Humbert' to the right of 2. Place the taller plant at the back and tilt the plant forward to the left.

4. Divide the 'Dragon's Blood' in two and plant a segment next to 3. Let the stems hang over the front edge of the pot.

5. Tilt the Scapigera forward to the left so that the stems protrude over the front of the pot.

6. Divide the Batesii in two plants and place a segment behind and to the right of 5, surrounding 5.

7. Plant the 'Kakurei' in the center of the pot, tilted slightly to the left. Since the stem is tall, place it as far back as possible.

8. Plant Adolfi to the right of Scapigera, taller stems behind shorter ones.

9. Divide the Athorum in two and plant a segment next to 8. Let the stems hang down in front of the pot.

10. Plant 'Queen Red' at the far right of 9. Place the flower spikes and the cluster slightly to the left.

11. Plant the remaining Remota to the right front of 10, with the stems hanging over the edge of the pot.

12. Plant the remaining Batesii to the right of 10. Some stems should hang over the right front edge.

(13) Plant the Undulatum at the back of the Batesii.

(14) To the right of the Undulatum, plant the remaining 'Dragon's Blood' to make the base of the Undulatum more spectacular.

(15) Plant 'Scheideckeri' at the front right end, placing it so that the leaves hang over the front edge.

Finished

(16) Plant the remaining Athorum at the far right of 15 to complete the arrangement.

Tip 1: Layout to create a natural atmosphere.

Before planting, decide the approximate layout. Place the taller plants in the back, medium-sized ones in the middle, and the short ones in the front. To avoid a rigid appearance, do not place tall plants symmetrically on both sides or at the center; instead, slightly offset them from the center. Tilt the 'Kakurei' to the left and direct the flower spikes of 'Queen Red' to the left as well for a more natural look.

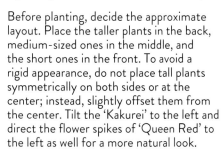

Tip 2: Make movements with drooping varieties of succulents.

Medium-height plants like Echeveria macdougalii, 'Yellow Humbert', and 'Queen Red' help add volume to the arrangement. Shorter plants such as 'Scheideckeri' and Kalanchoe scapigera can be placed in the front or between taller and medium-sized plants to fill in the space and achieve balance. Varieties with small leaves and drooping stems should be planted in the front, with the stems hanging outward to create movement.

FEBRUARY | C. Simple Style with a Scandinavian Feel

Materials for this group planting

Layout

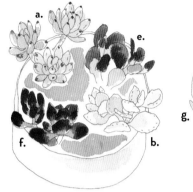
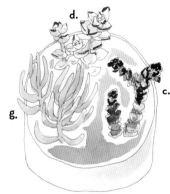

Plants

a. Sedum 'Alice Evans'

b. Kalanchoe millotii
★ Alternate =
Kalanchoe bahatii

c. Crassula 'Jade Necklace'
★ Alternate = Crassula
perforata

d. Crassula conjuncta

e. Senecio
jacobsenii

f. Crassula atropurpurea
var. watermeyeri
★ Alternate = Velutina

g. Senecio antandroi
★ Alternate = Senecio
serpens

Pot

Gray ceramic pot:
Diameter 4.25" (110mm) x Height 5.5" (140mm)

How to Plant

(1) Plant 'Alice Evans' in the back left of the pot. Tilt the plant outward to create a higher center and give the plant a spreading appearance.

(2) Plant Watermeyeri in the front left. As with 1, tilt the plant outward.

(3) Plant the main plant, 'Millotii', in the right front. Tilt the plant outward and make the center higher.

Finished

(4) Plant Jacobsenii in the back right. Surround the main plant with red foliage varieties to emphasize its presence.

(5) Plant the other grouping in the same way, following the illustration above.

Tip 1: Tilt the seedlings to adjust the height of the arrangement.

This arrangement utilizes varieties with different leaf shapes and growth habits, creating a contrast between round and linear in two matching points. The trick to a beautiful side-by-side display is to ensure that the arangements have similiar heights and sizes when finished. The taller succulent, Senecio antandroi, is planted in the left front to balance with the others.

Tip 2: Play up the differences in leaf color and leaf shape.

In one pot we are planting succulents with round-shaped leaves, alternating leaf colors between silver and those that turn pink in cold temperatures. The other pot features Senecio antandroi, which has long, narrow leaves with bluish tints. We use 'Jade Necklace' with its reddish tips as an accent. The plants we've chosen for this pot grow upwards to emphasize the vertical lines.

What are succulents?

Succulent plants are drought-resistant and come in various shapes and forms. Let's explore their characteristics.

Succulent Growing Environments Around the World

Succulents are plants that have the ability to enlarge their leaves, stems, and roots to store water. Their native habitats include dry regions with distinct dry and rainy seasons, such as South Africa, East Africa, Madagascar, and Central and South America. It is said that there are around 10,000 species of succulent plants that grow naturally in these areas.

Succulents can be found in all but the most inhospitable, barren parts of the world. They fall into two basic growth types—those that grow during the warmer months and go dormant in the cold seasons, and those that grow in winter.

Types and Characteristics of Succulents

Succulents have adapted their forms to their native habitats, resulting in a great variety of leaf shapes, textures, colors, and forms. Some have round, elongated, flat, small, or large leaves.

Some plants are tall while others have slow-growing rosettes. Some have dynamic growth while others cascade or sprawl. The fun of succulents is that you can combine these diverse and unique plants to create beautiful original arrangements.

Understanding the Nature of Succulents

Succulents native to arid regions have excellent water storage capabilities, are tolerant of drought and dislike excessive humidity. They prefer sunny, well-drained and well-ventilated locations. However, some, such as Haworthia, are susceptible to leaf burn when exposed to strong outdoor sunlight. These varieties are best grown on balconies or indoors where they can avoid direct sunlight. High temperatures and high humidity are challenging for any succulent and can lead to rot.

Summer growth type
These plants grow from spring to fall and take a break from growth in winter. Most of the succulents commonly available, including Echeveria, Graptopetalum, Pachyphytum, and Sedum, are summer-hardy genera.

Peach Pride

Winter-growing type
These plants grow from fall to winter and take a break from growth in the summer. Some examples include Aeonium, Otona, Senecio, Lithops, Conophytum, and Crassula.

Aeonium arboreum 'Zwartkop'

MARCH

Floral Beauty to Preface Spring
A Cold-resistant Sempervivum Arrangement

The star of this month's show is Sempervivum, with rosette-shaped leaves that are lovely as flowers. By just changing the style of the pot you use to display them, they will display a variety of charming expressions.

A. Get Creative with Everyday Items

Enjoy the remnants of winter foliage with a Japanese-style garden of Sempervivum

Semperivum (commonly known as "Hens and Chicks") shows beautiful leaf colors during its growth periods in spring and fall, and in winter, it turns a dark reddish hue due to the cold. It is highly resilient to cold and can survive outdoors during winter, but it doesn't fare well in hot and humid conditions. During summer, it should be kept in a semi-shaded outdoor area with little rainfall to keep it slightly dry. In spring and fall, water generously when the surface of the soil becomes dry.

This arrangement using a wok with holes at the bottom was created to resemble a miniature garden. A rock is placed in the center, and the plants are arranged around it to create an artistic composition, giving it the look of a Japanese garden. While freshly-purchased plants can make a beautiful arrangement, I prefer the appearance of the plants that have been around a while. As the roots grow firmly and numerous small offsets develop around the parent plant, the natural growth is impressive and touching.

Main plant: Sempervivum cv. 'Grass'
Supporting plant: Sempervivum cv. 'Blue Boy'

Characteristics of Spring Succulents

As the weather gradually becomes warmer, the growth of spring and fall-type succulent plants begins. The leaf colors, which were tinted by the cold, change to fresh and vibrant hues in spring. The shipment of Sempervivum seedlings is most common from March to May. By April and May, spring is in full swing, and garden centers are filled with a variety of colorful succulent plants.

First, decide on the placement of the
rocks. Place them slightly back from
the center to give the plants ample
space in the front. Expanding the
front space creates a sense of depth.

Once the *Senico radicans* (String of Bananas) and *Othonna capencis* 'Ruby Necklace' have grown, trim them at the base to reduce the number of stems. As they are easy to root, it is advisable to propagate them through cuttings.

B. Elegantly Planted Like a Bouquet of Flowers

Rounded and rounded
Make it look like a gorgeous bouquet

Create a bouquet of Sempervivum flowers in a variety of colors such as green, deep red, and silver with a hint of blue. Long-stemmed *Senecio radicans* (String of Bananas) and *Othonna capencis* (Ruby Necklace) are planted between the plants to add a touch of glamor. Temperatures of 41°F (5°C) or lower will damage String of Bananas and 'Ruby Necklace', so place them outside under a well-lit eave and keep them slightly dry.

Main plant: : Sempervivum 'TL'
Supporting plant: Sempervivum arachnoideum

Recreate native landscapes in a little angel pot

Inspired by the appearance of sempervivum growing in clusters in their native habitat, we planted some in a pot adorned with an angel.

   The reddish accents from *Sedum spurium* 'Tricolor' add movement. If you want to plant Sempervivum alone, you can place your arrangement in an uncovered area, but since we have added *Crassula remota* and *Sedum rubens*, it is best to keep it a dry area under a well-lit eave.

Main plant: Sempervivum cv. 'Oubeni-makiginu'
Supporting plant: Sedum spurium 'Tricolor'

In the summer, reduce watering and keep it on the dry side. You can either thin the branches from the base of the plant to improve air circulation or reduce the number of plants before the rainy season starts, and it's also good to re-trim and reshape them.

Materials for this group planting

Layout

Plants

a. Sempervivum 'Gazelle'

b. Sempervivum 'Shanghai Rose'

c. Sempervivum cv. 'Blue Boy'
★ Alternate = Echeveria 'Mira'

d. Sempervivum cv. 'Grass'
★ Alternate = Echeveria 'Raspberry ice'

e. Sempervivum 'Bronco'

f. Sempervivum ossetiense

Pot

Chinese wok:
Diameter 12" (305 mm) x Height 2.75" (70 mm)
Rock: Width approx. 6" (150mm) x Depth 3" (80mm) x Height 3" (80mm)
Culture medium for succulents (to decorate the soil)

How to Plant

1 Fill the container with large akadama pebbles (commercially available drainage pebbles can also be used).

2 Place the rock and seedlings in the container and determine the approximate arrangement.

3 Fill the container with soil, and plant the Ossetiense and the 'Shanghai Rose' at the far left.

4 Place the rock in front of 3 and bury it about halfway under the soil to secure it.

5 Plant 'Gazelle' in the left front of the container.

6 Plant the 'Grass' in the most prominent position near the center.

7 Plant the 'Bronco' in front of the 'Grass'.

8 Plant the 'Blue Gay' next to 'Grass'. Note how the blue-leafed and green-leafed succulents complement the red.

9 Add succulent culture medium (instead of decorative gravel) to cover the soil.

Finished

Tip: Drill a hole in the bottom of the pot to make an original container.

The pot used for this arrangement is an iron two-handled wok, beautifully simple in form. When using household items as pots, I try to first add holes to the bottom with an electric drill whenever possible. If it's not possbile to drill holes, be sure to add a root rot inhibitor after setting pebbles in the bottom of the pot.

MARCH | B. Elegantly Planted Like a Bouquet of Flowers

Materials for this group planting

Layout

Plants

a. Sempervivum
arachnoideum
★ Alternate = 'Gazelle'

b. TL
Sempervivum 'TL'
★ Alternate = 'Bronco'

c. Sempervivum
'Black Prince'

d. Sempervivum
'Woolcott's Variety'

e. Othonna capencis
(Ruby Necklace)

f. Sempervivum
'Firebird'

g. Sempervivum
'Uranus'

h. Senecio radicans
(String of Bananas)

Pot

Moss pot: Diameter 9.5" (240mm) x Height 9" (230mm)

How to Plant

1. Lay out the seedlings to be used for mixtures and determine the approximate arrangement.

2. Raise the soil in the center. Plant the 'Firebird' in upper left, tilting it outward.

3. Divide the Radicans in two and plant a segment in front of 2, with the stems cascading from the edge of the pot.

4. Plant the Arachnoideum in front of the 'Firebird', tilting the plant outward.

5. Plant the remaining Radicans to the right of the Arachnoideum.

6. Divide the Capencis in two and plant a segment in front, with the stems cascading from the edge.

7. Plant the 'Black Prince' in the center, ensuring that it's the highest point of the arrangement.

8. Tilt 'TL' outward toward the front and plant the remaining Capensis to its right.

9. Plant the 'Woolcott's Variety' at the far right, tilting it outward.

10. Plant 'Uranus' in the back, tilting it outward.

11. Arrange stems of the Radicans and Capensis to create a sense of movement.

Finished

MARCH | C. In Pots with Lots of Personality Use Lots of Volume

Materials for this group planting

Layout

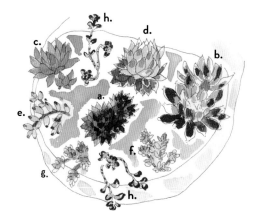

Plants

a. Sempervivum cv. 'Greenland'

b. Sempervivum cv. 'Oubeni-makiginu'
★ Alternate = 'Shanghai Rose'

c. Sempervivum 'Grey Dawn'

d. P. Sempervivum cv. 'P. Tuberosum'

e. Sedum rubens

f. Sedum orostachys

g. Crassula remota

h. Sedum spurium 'Tricolor'
★ Alternate = 'Dragon's Blood'

Pot

Pot:
Diameter 8.25" (210mm) x 4.75" (120mm).
With decorative figure, Width app 10" (250mm) x Height 11" (280mm)

How to Plant

① Lay out the seedlings and determine their approximate placement.

② Fill the container with potting pebbles and soil.

③ Plant the 'Grey Dawn' at the left edge, tilted outward, with stems protruding from the edge.

④ Divide the 'Tricolor' into two segments and plant one next to 3.

⑤ Plant the Rubens in the front, hanging over the edge, and 'P. Tuberosum' higher in the back.

⑥ Plant 'Greenland' in the center slightly elevated, and Remota in the front, with stems hanging over the edge.

⑦ Plant the remaining 'Tricolor' flanking 6, with stems hanging over the edge.

⑧ Plant Orostachys next to 7, stems pointing outward.

⑨ Plant the 'Oubeni-makiginu' on the far right. The plant should be tilted outward and low to the surface.

Finished

Tip: How to divide plants without damaging the roots.

Hold the base of the plant and divide slowly. Plants with delicate roots like Echeveria, Sedum and Sempervivum need extra care. Plants like Haworthia, Agave and Aloe have thick roots and separate offshoots, so are easier to divide.

APRIL

Springtime Groupings in Serene Pastel Tones

The long-awaited arrival of spring is in full swing. We have created a spring-colored collection of pale-toned succulents. The pale colors of the leaves look lovely in the gentle sunlight.

A. Fresh Green Gradation

Enjoy the arrival of spring with fresh green leaves

In April, succulents that were deeply tinted in fall hues during winter take on fresh, vibrant colors, and many varieties are in a period of substantial growth.

For spring, fall, and summer types, it is also the season for repotting and re-tailoring.

I made this refreshing pale-toned wreath with the hope of creating an assembly that would look good in the warm spring sunlight. I used green succulents with leaves ranging from dark green to light green and light yellow, with a gradation of colors in mind.

The wreath frame is also painted in pastel green to add even more freshness to the overall look. As the temperature rises, the plants will grow more vigorously, so be sure to trim the stems that extend beyond the wreath every month to maintain that nice round shape.

Main plant: Sedeveria 'Supar Brow'
Supporting plant: Echeveria 'Van Breen'

SUCCULENT

Plant the seedlings so that they don't extend too far beyond the wreath's edge. In spring, place in full sun and water generously when the soil dries out. In mid-summer, keep the wreath in a well-ventilated, half-shaded area and water moderately. Around October, combine pruning with low-growing plants to redesign the arrangement.

Be moderate when watering pots without drainage holes, ensuring that the soil dries out slightly after a day or two. The dryness of the soil may vary depended on placement and weather, so check the soil now and then and adjust your watering accordingly.

B. An Arrangement of Impressive Delicateness

Sedum's lovely new leaves are like a fresh salad

This arrangement was inspired by a fresh green salad. It's perfect for April and May, when the the new leaves show especially beautiful colors. *Echeveria* 'Perle Von Nurnberg' was chosen to give the different shape of Sedum even more impact and enhance the overall loook. For indoor care, make sure to provide sufficient light and ventilation to prevent elongation. I recommend managing the arrangement in an outdoor location with good sunlight exposure, such as a balcony or under the eaves, where it won't be exposed to rain.

Main plant: Sedum adolphi
Supporting plant: Echeveria 'Perle Von Nurnberg'

With Rubrotinctum and Prolifera
Make the base of the plant strong and lush

With the soft velvety texture of *Kalanchoe behalensis* 'Fang' and the slightly pinkish hue of *Aeonium urbicum* 'Sunburst' it's fun to try creating a feminine world in matching tins. Plant *Sedum prolifera* and *Sedum rubrotinctum* f. *variegata* at the base of the long, slender stems of 'Sunburst' and 'Fang'. Maintaining a low plant height will enhance the arrangement's beauty. Observe and prune to keep the desired height.

Main plant: Kalanchoe behalensis 'Fang', Aeonium urbicum 'Sunburst'
Supporting plant: Sedum prolifera, Pachyveria 'Blue Mist'

Avoid direct sunlight in midsummer, as it may lead to leaf burn. Water sparingly in mid-summer and mid-winter, and generously in spring and fall when the soil surface is dry.

41

APRIL | A. A Fresh Green Gradation

Materials for this group planting

Layout

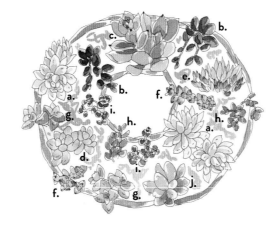

Plants

c. Echeveria 'Van Breen'
★ Alternate = Echeveria 'Midoribotan'

a. × Sedeveria 'Supar Brow'
★ Alternate = Sedum morganianum

b. Senecio rowleyanus

d. Sedum treleasei

e. Orostachys japonica

f. Crassula 'Tom Thumb'

j. Pachyphytum compactum

g. Crassula rupestris cv.

h. Crassula 'David'

i. Sedum makinoi

Pot

Wicker wreath form:
Diameter 9" (230mm) x Planting width 2.75" (70mm) x Height 2.75" (60mm)
Moss/Acrylic paint (pastel green)/Brush

How to Plant

1. Paint the entire wreath stand with pastel green acrylic paint.

2. Punch holes in the plastic lining.

3. Fill with soil. Since the planting area is shallow, you do not need to use potting pebbles.

4. Fill to about an eighth of capacity.

5. Plant the 'Van Breen'. Keep the plant perpendicular to the soil and do not extend beyond the edge.

6. Divide the Rowleyanus in two and plant a segment beside 1, overhanging the inner edge.

7. Plant the 'Supar Brow' in front of 6. Plant the seedlings in the front and back, shifting them around.

8. Plant the two divided Rupestris along the outer edge.

9. Divide the Makinoi in two and plant a segment behind 8 along the inner edge.

10. Plant Treleasei next to the Makinoi.

11. Divide 'Tom Thumb' in two and plant a segment next to the Treleasei.

12. Divide 'David' into two and plant a segment next to the 'Tom Thumb'.

How to Plant

(13) Plant the remaining Rupestris next to the 'David'.

(14) Plant the Compactum in the center of the planting area next to the Rupestris.

(15) Plant the remaining Makinoi, spreading the plants to the width of the planting area, next to 14.

(16) Plant another segment of 'Supar Brow' diagonal to the one in 7.

(17) Plant the remaining 'David' on the outside edge next to the 'Supar Brow'.

(18) Plant the remaining 'Tom Thumb' on the inner edge behind the 'David'.

(19) Plant the Japonica next to the 'Tom Thumb'.

(20) Plant the remaining divided Rowleyanus next to the Japonica.

(21) Cover the soil with moss.

Finished

Tip: Contrasting foliage colors for a more expressive appearance.

Alternate large-leafed plants such as Compactum, 'Supar Brow', and 'Van Breen' with smaller-leafed plants such as Makinoi, Rupestris, and 'David'. In addition, try to alternate between darker and lighter colored plants. The difference in size and color will create a strong, expressive look.

APRIL | B. An Arrangement of Impressive Delicateness

Materials for this group planting

Layout

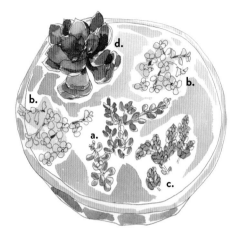

Plants

a. Sedum oryzifolium

b. Sedum makinoi 'Aurea'
★ Alternate = Sedum maakinoi 'Hosoba'

c. Sedum brevifolium

d. Echeveria 'Perle von Nurnberg'
★ Alternate = Graptoveria 'Douglas Huth'

Pot

Cafe au Lait Bowl:
Diameter 6" (150mm) x Height 3" (75mm)
Root rot inhibitor

How to Plant

1. Place root rot inhibitor in the bottom of the vessel.

2. Put drainage stones in the bottom of the pot.

3. Fill the container to about an eighth full with soil.

4. Plant 'Perle von Nurunberg' in the far left corner, tilting the seedling toward the edge of the pot.

5. Divide the 'Aurea' in about a 7:3 ratio and plant the larger segment in front of 4.

6. Hold the base of the Oryzifolium and spread the roots apart to widen.

7. Plant the Oryzifolium in the center of the container.

8. Plant the Brevifolium on the right.

9. In the empty space at the back of the bowl, plant the remaining 'Aurea'.

Tip: Changing the Shape of Plants.

Small-leafed species such as Sedum oryzifolium are essential as supporting plants in a group plant. They are often divided into two or three separate plants, but in this grouping I also altered a single plant. Hold the base of the plant with both hands and gently press down on the roots to spread them out.

Finished

APRIL | C. Showcasing the Charm of Succulents

Materials for this group planting

Layout

Plants

d. Kalanchoe beharensis 'Fang'
★ For replacemen = Beharensis whiteleaf

b. × Pachyveria 'Blue Mist'
★ Alternate = Pachyphytum compactum

a. Aeonium urbicum 'Sunburst'
★ Alternate = Moonburst

c. Sedum rubrotinctum f. variegata

e. Sedum porifera
★ Alternate = 'Little Beauty'

Pot

Square cans:
Large: Width 5" (125mm) x Depth 5" (125mm) x Height 7.75" (175mm)
Small: Width 4.25" (105mm) x Depth 4.25" (105mm) x Height 6" (150mm)
Moss / Root rot inhibitor

How to Plant

(1) Fill the can to one-fifth full with drainage stones.

(2) Add root inhibitor.

(3) Fill the pot to about four fifths full with potting soil.

(4) Plant the 'Sunburst' in the far right corner, tilting it slightly forward.

(5) Plant the 'Blue Mist' in the front left corner.

(6) Plant Rubrotinctum f. var. at the base of the 'Sunburst'.

(7) Cover the area where the soil is visible with moss.

Tip 1: Making a cohesive arrangement from multiple parts.

The two cans, one large and one small, are displayed side-by-side to show them as a single work of art. In both cans, the taller plants take the lead, with shorter plants added around their bases. The planting technique is consistent for both. I covered the exposed soil with moss to create a gentle impression that complements the pastel colors.

Finished

Tip 2: Plant with the viewer's eye in mind.

When making a group planting, first consider where the front will be and where it will be viewed from. For this arrangement, we focused on the side view. The main 'Sunburst' plant is placed at the back of the can, slightly tilted toward the front to showcase its leaf shape and beautiful colors.

How to Choose Succulent Seedlings Well

Succulents are readily available at garden stores and home centers. When buying, it's important to choose healthy seedlings.

How to recognize good seedlings

The leaves are short and compact, and the plants are low in height. The leaf color is vibrant, and the characteristics of the variety are well-defined. The upward growth type has a stable base outward, causing their color to become lighter.

How to recognize bad seedlings

Some varieties have elongated and stretched stems. In environments with limited sunlight or poor ventilation, the leaves may spread too much, causing their color to become lighter/faded.

Select compact, well-colored plants from the lineup at the store.

When choosing good succulent plants from the lineup at a well-lit store, look for plants with vibrant colors and compact growth. Several points should be considered when selecting succulents from a nursery. First, observe the store's environment, the leaf color, leaf shape, and how compact the plants are. Succulents placed in a low-light or poorly ventilated environment tend to elongate and become leggy. The colors of the leaves and new shoots become pale, losing their original beauty, and the plants become stretched out. Once they reach this state, they cannot return to their original form. Avoid choosing elongated seedlings. Instead, select a store that places their plants in well-lit environments to ensure the best quality for your selection. If a seedling has become elongated during growth, you will need to cut it back to the point where the nodes are densely packed.

Kuroda Gardening Market.

At my shop, my staff and I create all the arrangements. We display them with miscellaneous goods to create a natural ambiance.

MAY

A Mixed Arrangement Perfect for Giving

How about a succulent arrangement as a gift for a birthday, wedding, or no reason at all? Let's put our hearts and souls into it and make it unique.

A. Prioritize Balance as if Picking Wildflowers

A mixed succulents arrangement created and given with love

Once you get familiar with making mixed plant arrangements, why not take on the challenge of creating one as a gift for someone special? Compared to typical flowers, succulent plants require less frequent watering and are less susceptible to pests, making them easy to care for, especially for gardening beginners. Whether in a casual style, a glamorous bouquet-like arrangement, or a jewelry-box-inspired display with gem-like succulents, let's create stylish arrangements that can be proudly displayed and cherished.

I found a basket in a Finnish style at a novelty shop. I used it to make an informal gift for a friend. Using bright green and yellow-green succulents, I expressed the beautiful freshness of May greenery. It creates a bright atmosphere, making you want to take this basket to a picnic.

Main plant: Crassula rupestris f.
Supporting plant: Sedum makinoi

As they grow and the stems elongate, prune and shape them. The cut stems can be used for propagation through cuttings. It's best to divide and re-arrange around September to October.

B. A Style Both Festive and Elegant

Create a classy yet upbeat bouquet-like arrangement that is elegant and celebratory

Using a large number of seedlings to make it more luxurious, this arrangement is reminiscent of a wedding bouquet. When planted without gaps, growth is slower than in a more spaced-out arrangement. When plants are densely packed, ventilation is poor, so it's important to avoid excessive moisture. Keep the arrangement in a well-ventilated, sunny place, away from rain to ensure that it stays relatively dry. When the stems grow long and lose their form, cut them back to shape.

Main plant: Echeveria runyonii 'Topsy Turvy'
Supporting plant: Graptoveria 'Debbie'

If summer humidity is a concern you can rearrange the plant in early July. Reducing the arrangement by one plant increases the space between plants and improves air circulation.

C. An Arrangement Like a Chic Jewelry Box

A small box that makes an impressive succulent display

This stylish succulent jewelry box is the perfect romantic gift. The star of the show is *Haworthia cooperii*, which sparkles like a lens when it catches the light. Only three seedlings were used, but the long stems of the *Ceropegia woodii f. variegata* draped in the front add elegance. Both of these can suffer from leaf burn in direct sunlight, so keep this arrangement in a well-ventilated, semi-shaded area.

Main plant: Haworthia Cooperii
Supporting plant: Ceropegia woodii f. variegata
(String of Hearts)

These plants can be cultivated in a well-lit indoor space, but they are sensitive to high temperatures and humidity. During the peak of summer, place them in as cool an environment as possible. Avoid direct sunlight, soften the light with curtains or similar, and keep watering to a minimum.

MAY | A. Prioritize Balance as if Picking Wildflowers

Materials for this group planting

Layout

Note: Plants concealed by the basket handle are indicated by letter, but are not shown in this illustration.

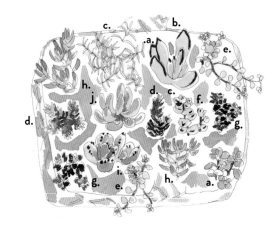

Plants

a. Sedum tetractinum

b. Cotyledon orbiculata

c. Sedum mexicanum

d. Villadia batesii

e. Sedum makinoi
★ Alternate = Sedum rupifragum

f. Crassula rupestris
★ Alternate = lupestris (Rupestris spp.)

g. Cremnosedum 'Little Gem'

h. Crassula mesembryanthemoides

i. Cotyledon tomentosa ssp. Ladismithensis

j. Pachyphytum hookeri

Pot

Woven basket:
W 8.25" (210mm) x D 6.75" (170mm) x
H 5.5" (140 mm) (Height to handle: 9" (230mm))
Plastic sheeting to line the basket
Root rot inhibitor

How to Plant

1. Roll up the plastic sheet and use a hole punch to make a hole in the part that will cover the bottom of the pot.

2. Spread sheet inside the basket.

3. Fill the basket with pebbles to about a tenth of the basket's depth.

4. Fill the basket to one-eighth full with soil.

5. Trim away any excess sheeting with scissors.

6. Divide the Mesembryanthemoides in two. Plant one segment at the back left corner with the stems leaning toward the edge.

7. Divide the Mexicanum in two. Plant a segment next to 6 with the stems leaning over the edge.

8. Divide the Makinoi in two and plant a segment to the right of and slightly higher than 7.

9. Plant the Hookeri to the right of the Mexicanum, perpendicular to the soil.

10. Divide the Batesii in two and plant a segment in front of 7. Lean the stems toward and over the edge.

11. Divide the 'Little Gem' in two and plant a segment to the left front, with the stems hanging over the edge.

12. Plant the Ladismithensis at the front.

(13) Divide the Tetractinum in two and plant a segment under the handles, directing the stems to the front.

(14) Plant the remaining Makinoi in the front and let the stems hang long over the edge.

(15) Plant the remaining Mexicanum under the handle.

(16) Plant the remaining Batesii in the center, perpendicular to the soil.

(17) Plant the remaining Mesembryanthemoides behind the Makinoi, tilting it toward the front.

(18) Plant the remaining Tetractinum to the right of 17. Tilt the seedlings toward the edge.

(19) Plant the Aiboshi at the back of 18. Plant Rupestris f. to the soil and taller than 17 and 18.

(20) Plant the Orbiculata at the back of 19.

(21) Plant 'Little Gem' to the right of 20 and the remaining Makinoi to the far right.

Tip: Choose lightweight soil and potting stones.

When using tawara or wooden baskets as pots, use a plastic liner with holes for drainage, these materials will rot if filled directly with soil. Furthermore, when using a less sturdy vessel like this basket, it is advisable to use a lightweight potting stone and soil to avoid increasing the weight as much as possible.

Finished

| # B. A Style Both Festive and Elegant

Materials for this group planting

Layout

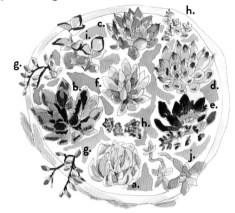

Plants

a. Echeveria runyonii 'Topsy Turvy'
★ Alternate = Lilacina

b. × Graptoveria 'Debbie'
★ Alternate = Chaviana

c. Echeveria 'Huthspinke'

d. Echeveria cv.

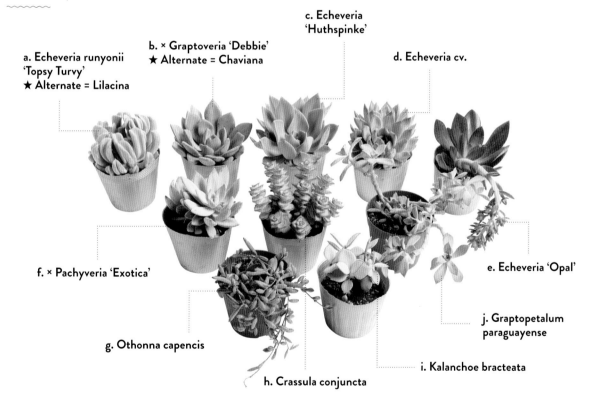

f. × Pachyveria 'Exotica'

e. Echeveria 'Opal'

j. Graptopetalum paraguayense

g. Othonna capencis

i. Kalanchoe bracteata

h. Crassula conjuncta

Pot

Patterned unglazed bowl:
Diameter 9" (230mm) x Height 7" (180mm)

How to Plant

① Place a potting net at the bottom, add pebbles to a tenth of the pot's depth, and soil to about four fifths.

② Plant the 'Huthspinke' in the back left, tilting the seedling toward the edge.

③ Divide Capencis in two and plant a segment, along with the Bracteata, in front of 2. Let the stems hang outward.

④ Plant 'Debbie' in the front left of the pot, tilting it toward the front.

⑤ Vertically place 'Exotica' in the center. Plant the remaining 'Ruby' in front and let its stems hang forward.

⑥ Divide the Conjuncta in two and plant a segment in front of 'Exotica' to contrast the foliage color and shape.

⑦ Plant 'Topsy Turvy' and Paraguayense in the front right. Let the Paraguayense hang over the edge for a dynamic effect.

⑧ Plant 'Opal' in the back right. To its left plant Echeveria cv., tilting it outward.

⑨ Plant the remaining Conjuncta in the center.

Tip: Add expression by contrasting colors and shapes.

To give the appearance of a bouquet, lean the seedlings at the edge of the pot slightly outward and plant taller plants in the center or elevate them by mounding the soil. Place the drooping-stemmed Capencis and vertically-growing Conjuncta to fill the spaces between the Echeverias, creating a contrast in the color and shape of the leaves.

Finished

MAY | C. An Arrangement Like a Chic Jewelry Box

Materials for this group planting

Layout

Plants

a. Adromischus
cooperi 'Tenkinshou'

b. Haworthia cooperi v
★ Alternate = Haworthia
Midoritama

c. Ceropegia woodii f. variegata
(String of Hearts)
★ Alternate = Ruby

Pot

Glass jewelry box:
3.5" (90mm) on all sides
Culture medium for succulents
Root rot inhibitor

How to Plant

1. Put root rot inhibitor in the bottom of the cube.

2. Fill the container to about seven eighths with soil for succulents.

3. Divide the Woodii f. var. into two and plant at the top left and bottom right corners.

Finished

4. Plant the main plant, Cooperi, at the front left, tilting it slightly toward the front.

5. Plant the 'Tenkinshou' at the back right and the rest of the Woodii at the front.

Tip: Keep the side view in mind.

Considering that the plant will be placed indoors, we planted this arrangement in a way that looks good from various angles. When using transparent glass as a container for small arrangements, the soil is visible, so choose one that looks good. Here we used a a fine-grained, blended culture soil formulated for cacti and succulents.

Oddballs are Part of the Family Too

A slightly eerie and unique grafted variety, a cactus with spines – these too are succulents.

Cacti are members of the succulent family

Succulents are plants that have roots, leaves, or stems that are swollen to store water, enabling them to withstand drought. Cacti, which are native to desert regions in North and South America, are also a type of succulent. The cactus family is a massive one with over 200 genera and more than 2,500 species. As a result, they are often treated separately from other succulents. Their shapes range from columnar to fan-shaped to spherical, and they come in various colors and types of spines, showcasing a rich variety.

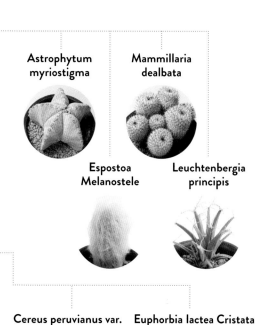

Astrophytum myriostigma

Mammillaria dealbata

Espostoa Melanostele

Leuchtenbergia principis

What is fasciation (or petrification)?

Plants typically grow upwards, with the growth point at the center. However, due to a mutation, sometimes this growth point develops horizontally, a phenomenon called 'cresting' or 'fasciation'. Crested succulents have shapes that differ from their regular forms, making them very intriguing and unique. Their strong visual impact makes them effective when used as focal points. Crested varieties used in this book include the 'Sunburst Crested' on page 85, and the *Cereus peruvianus var. monstruosus* and 'Cristata' on page 65.

Cereus peruvianus var. monstruosus

Euphorbia lactea Cristata (fasciation specie)

Although it has spines, it may not be cactus

Some succulents, such as the *Agave* 'Goshiki Bandai' or the Aloe *aculeata*, have spikes/spines similar to cacti. Among them, Euphorbia 'Kousaikaku' and 'Parida' in particular resemble cacti in shape. The difference between cacti and other succulents is that cactus thorns develop from an areola that looks fluffy like cotton, while other succulents do not have such areolas.

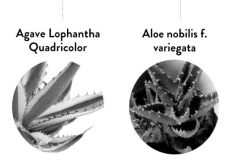

Agave Lophantha Quadricolor

Aloe nobilis f. variegata

JUNE

Cacti for Summer Group Plantings

Cacti are a very diverse group, numbering several thousand species in about 200 genera. Why not try some unique cacti in the hotter months of the year?

A. White Cactus with a French Shabby Chic Flavor

Shabby collection of white cacti

Cacti are a type of succulent.

During the growing seasons of spring and fall, expose them to direct sunlight outdoors. In the height of summer, avoid strong direct sunlight and afternoon sun, and place them in a bright semi-shade. They are sensitive to cold, so enjoy them by the window indoors during winter. Proper sunlight exposure in spring and fall, along with watering that doesn't overly dry the soil, will promote good growth.

Although cacti have a wild impression, some can be styled elegantly. For a decorative potted arrangement, we've only used white varieties. The lovely *Mammillaria geminispina* with its long spines and numerous offshoots, the beautifully-formed *Mammilaria dealbata*, the *Astrophytum myriostigma* and var. *Strongylogonum* with their white-speckled skin, and the *Mammillaria guelzowiana* covered in white spines have been used. Each brings its unique character. Experience and enjoy this arrangement that showcases each of their individualities.

Main plant: Astrophytum myriostigma
Supporting plant: Mammillaria dealbata

Characteristics of Succulents in Summer

In summer, many succulents that prefer strong light such as Aloes, Pachypodiums, Euphorbias and Sansevierias are available. They are tolerant of hot and humid summers and show off their beautiful greenery. Echeverias, Cassulas, Sedums, and Graptopetalums are also available, but in slightly smaller numbers than in spring and fall.

The growth of cacti is somewhat
slower compared to other succulent
plants. Depending on the growth
rate, if they seem cramped, consider
repotting them the following spring.

B. Have Fun with Masculine Styling

Matching pots and the plants in different flavors bring out the individuality of each

Display your favorite mini cacti in an antique pot: whether it's perfectly round, tall, fluffy with adorable white hair, or has a peculiar shape. Since the pot doesn't have drainage holes, be careful with watering. Use a watering can to give it a small amount of water or mist it lightly. Especially in the high temperatures of August, always ensure the soil doesn't stay constantly wet, as this can lead to root rot.

Main plant: Mammillariaplumosa 'Feather cactus', Espostoa Melanostele
Supporting plant: Crucigera, Lipsalis

Enjoy the variety in form and size of cacti in a mixed pot. Display with a rustic aesthetic.

C. Charming Cacti in a Yellow Bonsai Pot

Artistic fasciated cactus in a Japanese style

Combining the *Cereus peruvianus var. monstruosus* and *Cristata*, the crested cactus might seem a bit eerie at first glance. However, when paired with a yellow bonsai pot, it surprisingly fits in seamlessly. Additionally, two *Parodia leninghausii* are added to emphasize the yellow and green hues. As a finishing touch, white *Mamillaria bocasana* is placed in the front right, finishing off the arrangement with a Japanese flavor.

Main plant: Cereus peruvianus var. monstruosus
Supporting plant: Notocactus leninghausii

Best kept in direct sunlight for at least 6 hours a day. In spring and fall, water generously 2-3 days after the topsoil is white and dry. In the height of summer water once or twice a month on a cooler day.

JUNE | A. White Cactus with a French Shabby Chic Flavor

Materials for this group planting

Layout

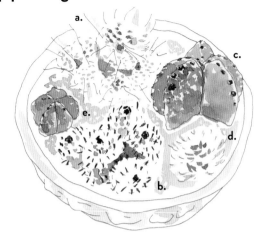

Plants

a. Mammillaria geminispina

b. Mammillaria dealbata
★ Alternate = Epithelantha 'Getsusekai'

c. Astrophytum myriostigma
★ Alternate = Astrophytumasterias 'Kabuto'

d. Mammillaria guelzowiana

e. Astrophytum myriostigma var. strongilogonum

Pot

Unglazed pot with patterned legs:
Diameter 10" (250mm) x Height 3.5" (90mm)
(Height including pedestal: 6.25" (160 mm)
Culture medium for succulents

How to Plant

1. Place a potting net on the bottom. Add pebbles and soil for succulents, and plant the Geminispina in the back center.

2. Plant the Dealbata in the front left corner. Arrange the seedlings so that the shorter ones are in the front.

3. Plant the Myriostigma in the back right.

4. Plant Strongilogonum next to the Myriostigma.

5. Place the Guelzowiana at the front right. All the cacti are planted vertically, creating a height difference by varying the height of the seedlings.

Finished

Tip: Coordinate with a single color to bring out the individuality of each variety.

Although the white varieties are coordinated, the monochromatic arrangement allows you to accentuate the characteristics of each variety, such as those with hairs, those that blow their offspring, and those that do not have stigmas. The first step in the arrangement is to decide on the location of the three key plants, Gemnispina, Dealbata, and Myriostigma, and then add small cacti between the plants.

JUNE | B. Have Fun with Masculine Styling

Materials for this group planting

Layout

Plants

a. Rhipsalis capilliformis
★ Alternate = Echinopsis chamaecereus 'Byakudan'

b. Espostoa ritteri
★ For replacemen = Espostoa melanostele

c. Leuchthenbergia principis 'Kousan'

d. Mammillaria crucigera
★ Alternate = Epithelantha micromeris var. ungnispina 'Kaguyahime'

e. Mammillaria theresae

f. Mammillaria plumosa 'Shiraboshi'
★ Alternate = Mammillaria hahniana 'Tamao'

Pot

Antique pot:
Diameter of planting area: 1.4–2" (35–50mm)
x Height: 4–4.75" (100–120mm) (6 pots)
Culture medium for succulents
Root rot inhibitor

How to Plant

1 Fill the pot one-third full with cactus soil.

2 Add root rot inhibitor.

3 Place the seedling in the pot, fill the space between seedling and pot with soil, and insert a thin stick to settle the soil.

4 Before planting larger-root plants, remove the soil from the roots.

5 Wear gloves when holding the cactus. Those without prickles may be worked with bare hands.

6 Lift the seedling slightly and fill the space in the pot with soil.

7 As in step 3, insert a thin stick into the pot to help the soil settle. Be careful not to damage the roots.

Finished

Tip: Repotting a Cactus

If the roots of the cactus have filled the pot, gently loosen and remove the attached soil. If the roots have grown too long, you can cut about a third of them with scissors. If you do this, don't replant immediately. Leave it for 1–2 days to let the cut end dry before planting.

JUNE | C. Charming Cacti in a Yellow Bonsai Pot

Materials for this group planting

Layout

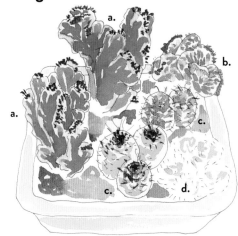

Plants

a. Cereus peruvianus var. monstruosus
★ Alternate = Cereus variabilis f. monstrosus 'Kinshishi'

b. Hildewintera aureispina f. cristata

d. Mammillaria bocasana

c. Parodia leninghausii
★ Alternate = Echinopsis calochlora 'Kinmaimaru'

Pot

Bonsai pot
Width 9" (230mm) x Depth 9" (230mm) x Height 3.5" (90mm)
(Height including legs 4.25" (110mm))

How to Plant

① Place a potting net in the pot.

② Fill the pot to one-fifth full with stones.

③ Add soil to up to about the last eighth of the pot's depth.

④ Plant one of the two var Monstrosus plants in the back left corner.

⑤ Plant the other plant in the front left, tilting it slightly forward.

⑥ Plant the Cristata at the far right.

⑦ Plant the larger of the two Leninghausii in the center.

⑧ Plant the other Leninghausii in front of 7, tilting it slightly forward.

⑨ Plant Bocasana in the front right.

Finished

Tip: After placement, allow the soil and seedlings to acclimate.

The most distinctive feature of cacti is their spines. Some have sharp tips, and some spines can easily come off and sting your hands, so always wear gloves when working with them.

After planting the cactus, lightly poke the soil with a stick. This will help the soil and roots to bond and firmly secures the plant in place.

JULY

Capture a cool summer moment with plants in a glass container

After the rainy spring season, the real summer arrives. I made a terrarium using a glass container to create a cooler impression amidst the hot and humid summer. It's okay to use familiar dishes or flower vases.

A. The Enduring Charm of Agave

The key to a container without a drainage hole is how you water

When I make a terrarium, I generally choose pots with drainage holes. However, if there is no hole, I try to create one if possible. For containers like the glass ones this month that can't have holes, I add anti-root rot agents when planting. The way you water a pot without holes is crucial. Always avoid a state where the soil is continuously wet. Water thoroughly only 2-3 days after the soil has dried out.

I used a transparent glass container for the Agave-focused terrarium. The layered soil and gravel inside seem like looking at a cross-section of the earth's strata. I've coordinated it with Agave, Haworthia, and Aloe, which grow well even indoors.

Main plant: ×Agave lophantha variegata
Supporting plant: Gasteraloe 'Manten no Hoshi'

If you're keeping this arrangement indoors, avoid places with intense western sunlight, as the container can become too hot. Adjust the environment by using items like lace curtains to block excessive light.

B. A Playful Arrangement in Bowls

Fresh salad-colored succulents

In bowls of the same shape but different colors, I've planted succulents in green and silver hues for a colorful arrangement. I used the same plants and kept the planting style consistent, emphasizing both continuity and cuteness. I chose varieties with soft hues, resulting in a cool and refreshing impression. After watering once, wait to water again until the soil is thoroughly dry. It's good to know how long it takes for the soil to dry out.

Main plant: Cotyledon undulata
Supporting plant: Sedeveria 'Yellow Humbert'

In July, the strong summer sunlight can cause leaf burn. Place in a well-ventilated semi-shade to avoid excessive heat, and manage accordingly.

C. Terrarium Focusing on the Beauty of Plant Form

A mini laboratory inside a glass vase

A thick, sturdy glass container gives a strong impression. In keeping with its elongated shape, I've chosen succulents that grow vertically. Branches and a thermometer give the arrangement a scientific feel.

As seedlings grow and stems become bushy, the inside of the vase can become cramped and may risk condensation. Trim stems from the base to reduce their number and create space inside the vase.

Main plant: Right: Aloe rauhii 'Dorian Flake'
Left: Sedum adolphii 'Golden Glow'
Supporting plant: Right: Crassula mesembryanthemoides
Left: Crassula cv. (Yoshitsune no mai)

Aloe plants produce offshoots around the parent plant. When they grow to the point of touching the glass, it's best to divide the plants in early fall.

JULY | A. The Enduring Charm of Agave

Materials for this group planting

Layout

d.

a.

b.

c.

Plants

a. Aloe nobilis variegata

b. Agave lophantha variegata
★ Alternate = Agave victoriae-reginae Moore

c. × Gasteraloe 'Manten no Hoshi'
★ Alternate = Aloe variegata

d. Haworthia reinwardtii var. chalwinii

Pot

Square glass base: Width 5.5" (140mm) x Diameter 5.5" (140mm) x Height 5.5" (140mm)
Pumice / Gravel / Small-grain akadama soi / Root rot inhibitor

How to Plant

1. At the bottom of the pot, place pumice and gravel, adjusting the thickness while tilting it.

2. On top of 1, fill the pot to eighty percent full with akadama soil.

3. Plant Lophantha var. in the left front. Align the seedling with the corner of the pot and tilt it toward the edge.

4. Place the 'Manten no Hoshi' to the right of the Agave. Seedlings should be aligned with the corners of the vessel, tilted toward the rim, with leaves facing outward.

5. Plant Nobilis var. at the far right.

6. Plant the Chalwinii in the back center.

Finished

Tip 1: How to repot thick-rooted plants.

When planting succulents with thick roots, like the Agave genus, remove the old soil thoroughly after removing the plant from its pot, being careful not to cut the roots. Though Agave is a very robust plant, it dislikes dry roots, so work quickly. The same goes for Haworthia and Senecio.

Tip 2: Use gravel or soil to create a stratified look.

For the display soil, use pumice, gravel, and small-grain akadama soil. First, lay about 1–2" (3–5 cm) of pumice at the bottom, then add ½–1" (2–3 cm) of gravel, and finally, pour in the akadama soil. Creating a slope for a cross-sectional stratified appearance is interesting. Excess water will drain to the bottom pumice layer, considering drainage.

JULY | B. A Playful Arrangement in Bowls

Materials for this group planting

Layout

Plants

a. Sedum makinoi f. variegata

b. × Pachyveria 'Exotica'

c. Kalanchoe tomentosa
(Panda plant)

d. Echeveria pulvinata 'Frosty'

e. Sedum reflexum
'Chameleon'

f. Senecio serpens

g. Cotyledon undulata
★ Alternate: = Cotyledon orbiculata

h. × Sedeveria 'Yellow Humbert'
★ Alternate: = Sedeveria 'Soft Rime'

i. Echeveria 'Golden Glow'

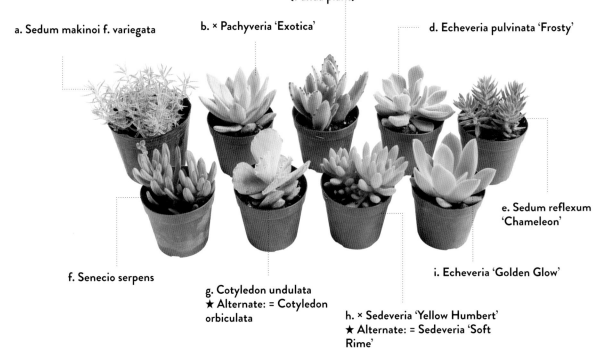

Pot

Glass bowl:
Diameter 6.25" (160mm) x Height 2.5" (65mm)
Growing medium for succulent plants / Root rot inhibitor

How to Plant

1 Add root rot inhibitor, potting stone, and soil, and plant the 'Exotica' in the back left corner, tilting it toward the edge.

2 Hold the base of the Makinoi f. var. plant and divide it into two plants.

3 In front of 1, plant one of the Makinoi segments, tilting it toward the edge.

4 Divide the 'Chameleon' into two plants and plant one to the left of 3. Plant the 'Golden Glow' on the inside.

5 In the front left corner, plant the main plant, the Undulata, tilting it toward the edge.

6 Plant 'Yellow Humbert' in the front right and the remaining Sedum in the back.

7 Plant the Tomentosa and 'Frosty' to the right of the Sedum. Plant the Kalanchoe perpendicular to the soil.

8 Plant the remaining 'Chameleon' in the back center.

9 Plant Serpens at the far right. The seedlings in the back should be planted upright so they can be seen from the front.

Finished

Tip: Deciding the placement before planting is crucial!

The main plant, Cotyledon, and the Kalanchoe, the point of interest, are both silver in color. To make them stand out, place them in the front and center. Next, the green 'Yellow Humbert' is placed to the right of the Cotyledon. Similarly, place the green 'Golden Glow' to the left rear of the Cotyledon. Finally, fill in the space between the plants with 'Chameleon' and Sedum.

JULY │ C. Terrarium Focusing on the Beauty of Plant Form

Materials for this group planting

Layout

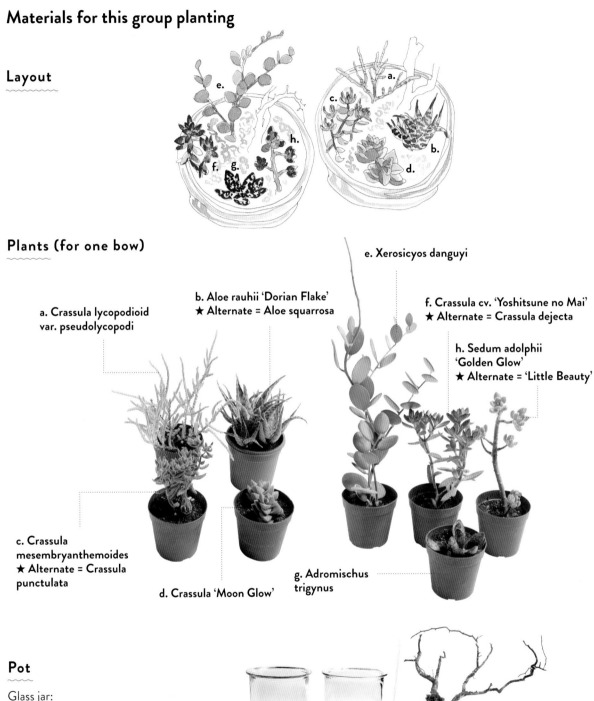

Plants (for one bow)

a. Crassula lycopodioid var. pseudolycopodi

b. Aloe rauhii 'Dorian Flake'
★ Alternate = Aloe squarrosa

e. Xerosicyos danguyi

f. Crassula cv. 'Yoshitsune no Mai'
★ Alternate = Crassula dejecta

h. Sedum adolphii 'Golden Glow'
★ Alternate = 'Little Beauty'

c. Crassula mesembryanthemoides
★ Alternate = Crassula punctulata

d. Crassula 'Moon Glow'

g. Adromischus trigynus

Pot

Glass jar:
Diameter 7.25" (185mm) x Height 9.75" (250mm)
Two branches / Thermometer for display
Culture medium for succulents / Root rot inhibitor

How to Plant

(1) Fill the container to one-third of its height with soil, add root rot inhibitor, and insert branches in the back.

(2) Plant the Danguyi beside the branch, using the branch as a support to make it stand.

(3) Plant 'Yoshitsune no Mai' on the front-left side.

Finished

(4) To the right of 'Yoshitsune no Mai' plant the 'Golden Glow'.

(5) In the foreground, plant the shortest plant, the Trigynus.

For the second group planting, follow the illustration (page 80) for plants **a.** through **d.**

Tip 1: Simple composition with a minimum number of seedlings.

Regardless of the composition, always decide on placement by sorting by tall, medium, and short plants. When there isn't much space for planting, keeping it simple with a minimum number of seedlings makes the process easier, ensuring all the plants stand out once the arrangement is complete.

Tip 2: Use branches to create a sense of unity and movement.

If it is difficult to create an atmosphere with succulents alone, you can create an interesting work of art by using branches. In this example, short branches are used on the right side of the glass, and long, curved branches are used on the left side of the glass. This adds cohesion and a sense of movement to the two compositions.

AUGUST

A Small Succulent Garden Enjoy Unique Forms on Your Midsummer Windowsill

The high temperature and humidity of midsummer are challenging for both people and succulents. We've gathered refreshing compositions suitable for indoor viewing by the window

A. Utilizing Sharpness for a Cool Look

Refresh a summer window with green succulents

The harsh heat of August tends to reduce gardening time, and direct summer sunlight can damage the plants. During this time, it's recommended to manage plants under eaves or indoors, away from direct sunlight. This month, create a composition to enjoy inside. A composition of Sansevieria featuring 'Mikado' and Francisii is chosen for their sharp forms. Emphasize the form of the Sansevieria by using a slender Omoto pot. The golden ratio of plant height to pot height is 1.5 to 2. Maintaining this ratio, even simple compositions will look stylish.

Furthermore, as Sansevieria is drought-resistant and sturdy, it's recommended for beginners. Position two pots of different sizes for a striking corner.

Main plant: large: Sansevieria bacularis 'Mikado' / small: Sansevieria francisii
Supporting plant: large: Sansevieria bella / small: Haworthia fasciata 'Juuni No Maki'

Protect from intense summer
sunlight and western sun as they
can cause leaf burn. Manage in
partial shade. *Haworthia fasciata
'Juuni No Maki'* and variegated
Senecio Rowleyanus need the
same care. They are somewhat
frost-sensitive; a temperature
above 41°F (5°C) is required for
overwintering.

B. Focusing on Balance

Enjoy the individuality of Haworthia's many forms

Haworthia are hardy and easy to grow and can be enjoyed indoors throughout the year.

When keeping them outdoors, it's best to place them under the eaves where they can avoid exposure to rain and direct sunlight during the growing season in spring and fall. In summer, or at any time of year, place them indoors on a windowsill.

Haworthia is a genus of infinite variety—colors from yellow-green to nearly black; patterns from solid to stripes and spots; broad leaves, narrow leaves, and lenses. There's even a fan-shaped variety among the vast number of rosette forms.

Above, eight varieties, including those with variegated patterns, yellowish-green colors, and unique shapes, are planted in old baking molds.

Main plant: large: Haworthia 'Shukuen nishiki' / small: Haworthia 'Shinen'
Supporting plant: large: Haworthia 'Gyokro' / small: Gasteria liliputana 'Kokame hime'

Place in it in a well-lit window and keep the soil on the dry side. Soil that is always moist can lead to root rot and ultimately kill the plant.

C. Enjoy Creating a Small Aquarium

Disused vessels make fantastic canvases for arrangements

Here we created an under-the-sea look with succulents mimicking aquatic plants in a vintage aquarium. If you look in antique shops or flea markets, you may be able to find many different types of old glassware. Reusing old containers can result in fasciniating compositons. Adjust the size of the *Sedum burrito* plant by cutting the the base as it grows.

Main plant: Aeonium urbicum 'Sunburst' f. cristata
Supporting plant: Crassula 'Tom Thumb'

Except for Sansevieria, during the hot summer months, they enter a dormant period, so reduce watering and keep them dry. From late September, increase the amount of water.

AUGUST | A. Utilizing Sharpness for a Cool Look

Materials for this group planting

Layout

Plants

a. Sansevieria francisii
★ Alternate = Lobster Flower

b. Haworthia fasciata 'Juuni No Maki'
★ Alternate = 'Juuni No To'

e. Sansevieria bacularis 'Mikado'
★ Alternate = Sansevieria stuckyi

d. Sansevieria bella
★ Alternate = Sanseviera patens

c. Senecio rowleyanus f.variegata (variegatad String of Pearls)

Pot

Omoto pot:
Large / Diameter 7.25" (185mm) x Height 7" (180mm); Small / Diameter 6.25" (160mm) x Height 6" (155mm)

How to Plant

(1) Place a potting net in over the drainage hole.

(2) Fill the pot to about a tenth of capacity with pebbles.

(3) Fill the pot halfway with soil.

(4) At the back left of the small pot, plant the Francisii perpendicular to the soil.

(5) Plant the Fasciata in the right front. Tilt the seedling toward the rim, with the leaves facing outward.

(6) Plant the Rowleyanus f. var. in the front left. Let the stems hang outward.

Finished

(7) Plant the 'Mikado' in the back left corner of the large pot.

(8) Plant Bella in the front right. These leaves have movement, so you'll want to find the most beautiful orientation before planting.

Tip: Sansevieria, a group of plants rich in individuality.

Sansevieria is a member of the Ranunculaceae family, with about 70 species found mainly in Africa, South Asia, and Madagascar. They are popular as houseplants, and in addition to the 'Mikado' and Francisii we used, many other varieties are available. From top left to right: Stuckyi, Francisii, Sparba, Bella, and 'Mikado'.

AUGUST | B. Focusing on Balance

Materials for this group planting

Layout

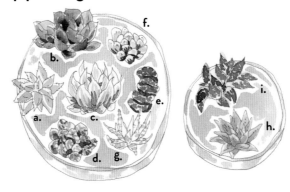

Plants

a. Haworthia cv. 'Lettie'

b. Haworthia cuspidata 'Takaragusa'

c. Haworthia turgida f. variegata 'Shukuen Nishiki'
★ Alternate = Haworthia 'Kagyo'

d. Haworthia obtusa var. pilifera 'Gyokuro'
★ Alternate = Haworthia obtusa

e. Haworthia truncata 'Gyokusen'

h. Haworthia cv. 'Shinen'
★ Alternate = Haworthia 'Manda's Hybrid'

f. Haworthia obtusa

g. Haworthia fasciata f. variegata 'Hakuchou'

i. Gasteria liliputana 'Kokame hime'
★ Alternate = Ernesti minima

Pot

Baking Molds:
Large / Diameter 7.5" (190mm) x Height 2.25" (60mm); Small / Diameter 3.75" (95mm) x Height 2.25" (60mm)
Root rot inhibitor / Silvery thread moss

How to Plant

① Put a shallow layer of soil in the pot and add root rot inhibitor.

② Start with three large seedlings. Plant the 'Takaragusa' at the left back.

③ Plant 'Shukuban Nishiki' in the center and 'Lettie' in the front left.

④ Plant 'Gyokuro' and 'Hakuchou' in the front.

⑤ Plant 'Gyokusen' to the right of the 'Hakuchou'.

⑥ Plant Obtusa to the far right of the 'Gyokusen'.

⑦ Cover the area where soil is visible with Silvery thread moss.

⑧ In the small container, plant the 'Kokame hime' on the left, perpendicular to the soil.

⑨ On the right, plant the 'Shinen' perpendicular to the soil.

Tip: Color contrast and height differences should be considered in the arrangement.

This arrangement is primarily composed of Haworthia plants, using varieties with different shapes and colors. Pair variegated ones with green leaves, and then lime green ones, and so on. Keep the soil flat, and create height differences using the plants themselves. Place smaller plants near the edge or next to larger plants for a natural look.

AUGUST | C. Enjoy Creating a Small Aquarium

Materials for this group planting

Layout

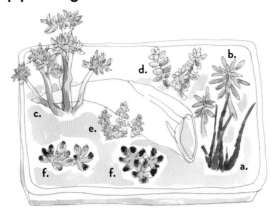

Plants

a. Sansevieria bacularis 'Mikado'

b. Echeveria 'Spruce Oliver'

c. Aeonium urbicum 'Sunburst' f.cristata ★ Alternate = Aeonium haworthii 'Tricolor'

d. Sedum burrito (Burrow's tail)

e. Crassula 'Tom Thumb' ★ Alternate = Crassula rupestris ssp.marnieriana

f. Sinocrassula densirosulata

Pot

Vintage aquarium:
Width 12" (305mm) x Depth 7.25" (185mm) x Height 8" (200mm)
(Height including legs 10" [250mm])
Two branches / Mountain moss / Humus/ Root rot inhibitor

How to Plant

(1) Fill the aquarium bowl with soil and root rot inhibitor.

(2) Arrange the branches before planting seedlings.

(3) Plant the Urbicum upright in the center left of the aquarium.

(4) Plant the two 'Spruce Oliver' at the back right, slightly tilted to the left.

(5) Plant the Burrito in the center back. It's unstable, so use a branch for support.

(6) Plant 'Mikado' in the front right, to create a contrast in shape with the Sedum.

(7) Plant the crassula in the right front of the Urbicum.

(8) Plant the Densirosulata, the shortest plant, in the left foreground.

(9) Cover the area where soil is visible with humus and mountain moss.

Finished

Tip: Create and enjoy a small landscape garden.

The entire surface is made of glass, allowing a clear view of the soil. The soil is elevated on one side and gently sloping on the other to create a natural atmosphere. Placing tree branches adds to the ambience and makes arranging the plants easier. The soil surface should be partially covered with mountain moss or fine humus for a natural look.

SEPTEMBER

Add Color and Boldness to Your Garden with Wide-Sized Group Plantings

Large arrangements are eye-catching and perfect for entrances or focal points in gardens. Use a large-sized pot for a dynamic arrangement. Add boldness and color to your garden by making your arrangement wide as well as tall.

A. A Bold Container Acts as a Focal Point

A large arrangement in a bold pot draws the eye to a given space

The large pot arrangements offer the appeal of using dynamic, impressive plants with strong presence not found in smaller seedlings. Despite the pot's size, the method and combination of plants remain the same as with smaller arrangements. Utilize bold forms and pot shapes to create unique arrangements.

This arrangement uses the prominent *Aloe dicotoma* as the main tree. The pot is a wooden barrel available at antique markets. Placing it at the entrance or other prominent spot anticipates the reactions of visiting guests. This time, Aloe is the main focus, but Agave, Kalanchoe, and Sansevieria are also recommended. Plants that have grown large often have interesting and unique shapes, so choose a plant that suits your own uniqueness.

Main plant: Aloe dichotoma
Supporting plant: Lomatophyllum prostratum

Place shorter plants around the main plant, making your arrangement lush at the base. In the height of summer, keep it semi-shaded and dry, move to a sunnier location around late September, and gradually increase watering. During winter, ensure it is kept in places where frost doesn't occur and the temperature remains above 41°F (5°C).

Plant mainly larger plants, high in the center and low at the edges. The drooping varieties are combined to create a bouquet.

B. Tilting the Seedlings to Create Rounded Shapes

Planting in a stately pot creates a sophisticated bouquet

The Echeverias with ruffled leaf edges are the centerpiece of the arrangement, and are joined by pale pink plants and some with flower spikes to create a rounded bouquet. This gorgeous arrangement makes a fantastic focal point in the garden.

To maintain its round bouquet shape, avoid plants that grow tall or change shape drastically after growth, and combine varieties with similar growth styles.

Main plant: Echeveria 'Early Light'
Supporting plant: Echeveria 'Domingo'

C. Large and Small Seedlings to Create an Impressive Three-Dimensional Effect

Taking advantage of the cart's shape and size, boldly place larger plants

This is a mixed planting in the wooden box part of the cart. It's still hot in September, but a large Echeveria with raised flower spikes is used as the main feature, coordinated in fall-like brown tones. It's finished in a dynamic style. With the large plants with raised flower spikes, balance with the patterned cart is achieved, creating movement. Medium to small succulents are planted in between the large ones, adding contrast and a three-dimensional feel.

Main plant: Aeonium 'Cashmere Violet'
Supporting plant: Echeveria 'Pallida'

Up to mid-September, when the heat lingers, manage like summer, in partial shade and slightly dry. After mid-month, when the sunlight mellows, place it in the direct sun outside. However, be cautious as sudden environmental changes can cause leaf burn.

SEPTEMBER | A. A Bold Container Acts as a Focal Point

Materials for this group planting

Layout

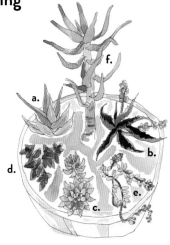

Plants

b. Lomatophyllum prostratum
★ Alternate = Tillandsia jucunda

a. Aloe ibitensis

c. Dudleya xantii

d. Crassula 'Shindou'

e. Sedum rubens

f. Aloe dichotoma
★ Alternate = Aloe plicatilis

Pot

Wooden barrel:
Diameter 12.5" (320mm) x
Height 12.5" (320mm)

How to Plant

1. Drill a hole in the bottom of the barrel, fill with potting stone and soil, and plant Dichotoma in the center back.

2. On the left side of the barrel, plant Ibitensis upright.

3. Plant the 'Shindou' in front of the Ibitensis, with the stems hanging outside the barrel.

4. To the right of 3, plant the Xantii, tilting toward the edge, allowing the stem to protrude outside.

5. To the right of 4, plant the Rubens, letting the stems hang outside.

6. Plant the Prostratum to the right of 5, tilting the plant toward the edge of the barrel.

Finished

Tip: Learn about the different types of hardy and unique aloe species.

It's good to familiarize yourself with the varieties of Aloe available to you. From the Barbadensis Miller so commonly known for its soothing properties to Dicotoma that can reach 33 feet (10 meters) in height, you'll discover a wide array of colors, shapes, sizes and textures in the over 300 varieties of Aloe known today.

SEPTEMBER | B. Tilting the Seedlings to Create Rounded Shapes

Materials for this group planting

Layout

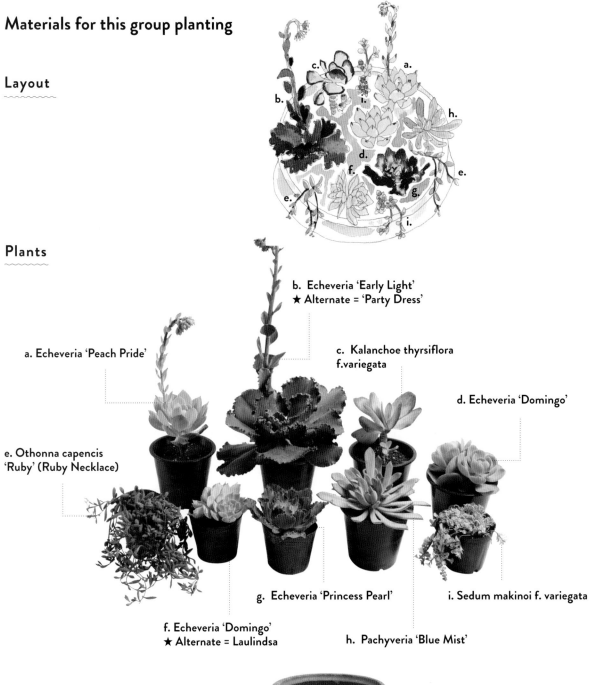

Plants

a. Echeveria 'Peach Pride'

b. Echeveria 'Early Light'
★ Alternate = 'Party Dress'

c. Kalanchoe thyrsiflora f.variegata

d. Echeveria 'Domingo'

e. Othonna capencis 'Ruby' (Ruby Necklace)

f. Echeveria 'Domingo'
★ Alternate = Laulindsa

g. Echeveria 'Princess Pearl'

h. Pachyveria 'Blue Mist'

i. Sedum makinoi f. variegata

Pot

Black pot:
Diameter 10.5" (265mm) x Height 8.25" (210mm)

How to Plant

① Plant the 'Early Light' in the far left corner of the pot. Tilt the seedlings outward.

② Divide the Capencis into two plants, and plant one in front of 'Early Light' with the stems hanging outward.

③ To the right of 2, plant 'Domingo'. The seedlings should be tilted outward.

④ Divide the Makinoi f. var. and plant a segment to the right of 3 making sure its hanging stem is shorter than that of 2.

⑤ Plant 'Peach Pride' in the center. The seedlings should be placed perpendicular to the soil.

⑥ Plant 'Princess Pearl' and the remaining Othonna to the right of 4.

⑦ Plant the 'Blue Mist' to the right of 6. Tilt the seedlings outward.

⑧ Plant another 'Peach Pride' next to 7.

⑨ Plant the remaining Makinoi and the Thyrsiflora at the back.

Finished

Tip: Arrange plants so that they are contrasting yet harmonious.

Before planting, arrange the seedlings next to each other and determine their placement. Focus on contrasting colors and shapes. I use both large and small Echeveria plants, and place them so that they form a nice circle when viewed from above and from the side. The seedlings on the edges should be tilted outward, while the center should be planted with the soil elevated and the seedlings upright.

SEPTEMBER | C. Large and Small Seedlings to Create an Impressive Three-Dimensional Effect

Materials for this group planting

Layout

Plants

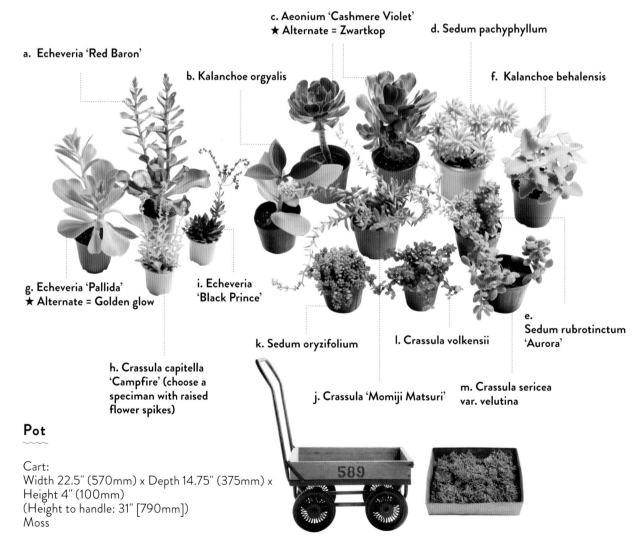

a. Echeveria 'Red Baron'

b. Kalanchoe orgyalis

c. Aeonium 'Cashmere Violet'
★ Alternate = Zwartkop

d. Sedum pachyphyllum

f. Kalanchoe behalensis

g. Echeveria 'Pallida'
★ Alternate = Golden glow

i. Echeveria 'Black Prince'

k. Sedum oryzifolium

l. Crassula volkensii

e. Sedum rubrotinctum 'Aurora'

h. Crassula capitella 'Campfire' (choose a speciman with raised flower spikes)

j. Crassula 'Momiji Matsuri'

m. Crassula sericea var. velutina

Pot

Cart:
Width 22.5" (570mm) x Depth 14.75" (375mm) x Height 4" (100mm)
(Height to handle: 31" [790mm])
Moss

589

How to Plant

1 Place a base net and potting stones at the bottom of the pot and fill it with soil up to 80 percent. Raise the center a bit higher with soil.

2 Plant the large seedlings first: 'Pallida' and 'Red Baron' at the left and right rear respectively.

3 Plant 'Campfire' between 'Pallida' and 'Red Baron'.

4 Plant Behalensis and Volkensii on the far left, with the Volkensii stems hanging over the edge.

5 Plant two 'Cashmere Violet' plants together in the most prominent spot of the front left corner.

6 Plant two divided Velutina plants at the base of the 'Cashmere Violet' plants.

7 Plant 'Aurora' in the center front, with the seedling tilted toward the front and the stem hanging over the edge..

8 Plant Orgyalis at the back right of 7, with the seedlings tilted slightly forward.

9 Plant the remaining Velutina and 'Black Prince' at the front right.

10 At the far right, plant the shortest plant, Oryzifolium, letting the stems hang over the edge.

11 Plant 'Momiji Matsuri' and Pachyphyllum behind 10.

Finished

OCTOBER

Create a Little World by Artistically Combining Seedlings

Succulents with unique and beautiful forms are works of art in themselves. Matching succulent plants with slightly unusual containers, we have created a world befitting the artistic fall season.

A. A Confined Space Made Soothing by Forest Objects

Placing succulents in an antique birdcage

To create an artistic arrangement in an antique birdcage that encloses succulent plants, it's essential to clarify the theme or the world you want to create. You should consider the pot you'll plant in and, if necessary, the atmosphere of the place where you'll put it, and then choose the seedlings. The chosen containers are an old birdcage, a large antique-style treasure box, and a pot that reminds one of a UFO in purple.

I took inspiration from a dense forest and captured the essence in a birdcage. With *Echeveria pallida* as the main plant, I added

others like *Aeonium arboreum* 'Zwartkop' and *Aeonium arboreum* to match the height of the cage, and *Echeveria pulvinata* 'Frosty' with its rising flower spike. Surrounding them with mid-to-low plants provides depth and height variations. Decorate with a small wooden bird as a perch, and you have a piece that brings a soothing, gentle atmosphere.

Main plant: Echiveria pallida
Supporting plant: Aeonium arboreum 'Zwartkop'

As the succulents will be viewed through the birdcage's grid, it's best to choose plants with round and/or large leaves so they won't blend in with the vertical lines of the mesh.

B. Treating the Succulents Like Jewelry is the Key

Sparkling succulents overflowing from a treasure box

The theme is a treasure chest found by pirates, with succulents resembling jewels overflowing from it. The primary point of this arrangement is choosing the variety of succulent plants. Small, drooping leaves of *Senecio rowleyanus* and *Sedum prolifera* are likened to necklaces, while silver succulents and colorful ones are treated as jewels. Adding decorative accessories enhances the treasure chest atmosphere.

Main plant: Sedum rubrotinctum 'Aurora'
Supporting plant: Othonna capencis 'Ruby'

The dynamic *Graptopetalum paraguayense* should be allowed to overflow boldly. As *Kalanchoe pumila* and *Sedum rubrotinctum* 'Aurora' grow, they will bring more movement.

104

Enjoy the collaboration of modern and natural

A modern purple pot is wrapped with grapevine for a natural look. *Echevieria* 'Afterglow' and *Echeveria* 'Mauna Loa', which turn red as the morning and evening temperatures drop, are given bold placement.

Intertwining the long stems of *Senecio rowleyanus* (String of Pearls) on the grapevine expresses artistic movement. The contrast of red, green, and silver captures the essence of autumn in one pot.

Main plant: Echeveria 'Afterglow'
Supporting plant: Echeveria 'Mauna Loa'

During the Echeveria's growing period, water generously once the soil surface has dried. Place it outside where it gets plenty of sunlight and good airflow.

Materials for this group planting

Layout

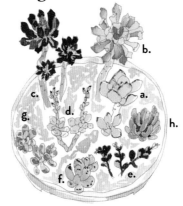

b.

c.

g.

d.

a.

h.

f.

e.

Plants

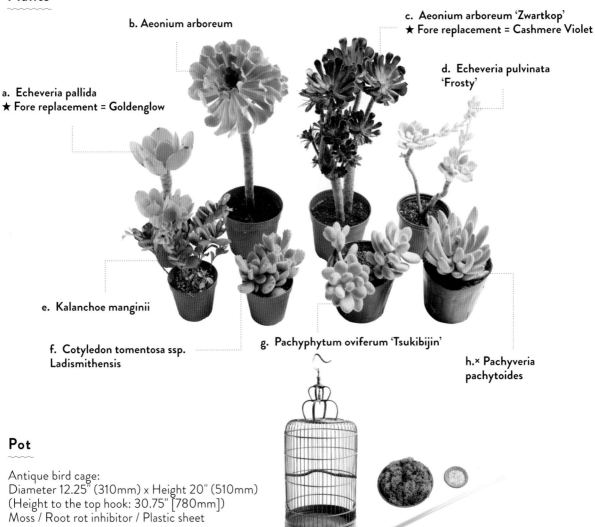

b. Aeonium arboreum

c. Aeonium arboreum 'Zwartkop'
★ Fore replacement = Cashmere Violet

d. Echeveria pulvinata 'Frosty'

a. Echeveria pallida
★ Fore replacement = Goldenglow

e. Kalanchoe manginii

f. Cotyledon tomentosa ssp. Ladismithensis

g. Pachyphytum oviferum 'Tsukibijin'

h.× Pachyveria pachytoides

Pot

Antique bird cage:
Diameter 12.25" (310mm) x Height 20" (510mm)
(Height to the top hook: 30.75" [780mm])
Moss / Root rot inhibitor / Plastic sheet

How to Plant

1. Spread a plastic sheet over the cage bottom and fill it with soil.

2. Cut the plastic sheet that protrudes from the container with scissors.

3. Plant 'Zwartkop' at the back of the container and 'Zwartkop' at the left front.

4. Plant Pallida between Arboreum and Zwartkop.

5. Plant 'Frosty' in front of 4.

6. Plant 'Tsukibijin' and the Ladismithensis in the left front.

7. Plant the Manginii to the right of the Ladismithensis.

8. Plant the Pachytoides to the right of the Magninii for color contrast.

9. Cover visible soil with moss to finish.

Finished

Tip: Water the plant by misting.

Water at the base of the plant with a spray bottle. Winter-type Aeonium that has been dehydrated during summer requires water around this time. Like other succulents, place it outside in a sunny location and gradually increase the amount of water. For this arrangement that has moss on the soil, water the moss with a spray bottle. Touch the soil with your fingers and check its dryness before watering.

OCTOBER | B. Treating the Succulents Like Jewelry is the Key

Materials for this group planting

Layout

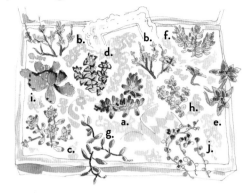

Plants

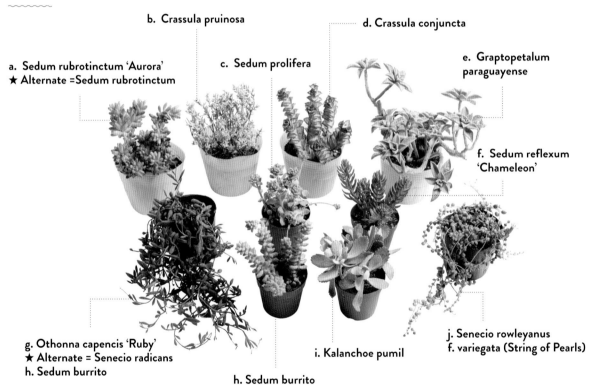

a. Sedum rubrotinctum 'Aurora'
★ Alternate =Sedum rubrotinctum

b. Crassula pruinosa

c. Sedum prolifera

d. Crassula conjuncta

e. Graptopetalum paraguayense

f. Sedum reflexum 'Chameleon'

g. Othonna capencis 'Ruby'
★ Alternate = Senecio radicans
h. Sedum burrito

h. Sedum burrito

i. Kalanchoe pumil

j. Senecio rowleyanus
f. variegata (String of Pearls)

Pot

Treasure chest-shaped box:
Width 16.5" (420mm) x Depth 11.5" (290mm) x
Height 5.75" (145mm)
Vinyl sheet / Display accessories
(2 candlesticks, 3 accessory boxes, picture frame)
Soil for succulent plants / Root rot inhibitor

How to Plant

1. Line the trunk with a plastic sheet.

2. Place a candle stand a bit towards the back right. Use taller items for the back.

3. Add root rot inhibitor and fill the trunk with succulent soil up to about eighty precent full.

4. Trim away overhanging plastic with scissors.

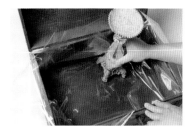

5. Place a picture frame in the back and partially bury it in the soil.

6. Tilt the candlestick downward and plant it in the center. Plant the 'Aurora' just in front if it, tilting it forward.

7. Plant the Conjuncta in front of the picture frame, tilting it slightly backward and to the right.

8. Divide the Purinosa in two and plant on the far left. Tilt the seedlings toward the edge.

9. Plant the Pumil in front of 8, and tilt the seedlings toward the edge as in 8.

10. Plant Prolifera in front of the left, with the seedlings leaning toward the edge and the stems hanging outward.

11. Plant 'Ruby' to the right of 10, stems hanging down in front.

12. Plant the remaining Purinosa to the far right of the 'Aurora'.

How to Plant

(13) In the right foreground, plant the Rowleyanus with stems hanging dover the edge.

(14) Plant Burrito at the far left of 13.

(15) Plant the Paraguayense at the far right of Burrito with the stems hanging outward to create a spreading effect.

(16) Plant 'Chameleon' at the far right. The seedlings should be slightly tilted toward the edge.

(17) Place display items in the empty space.

(18) Arrange some of the 'Ruby' stems by twisting them around the 'Aurora' and nearby display items.

Finished

Tip: Create a sparkling effect by mixing succulents with other items.

Water at the base of the plant with a spray bottle. Winter-type Aeonium that has been dehydrated during summer requires water around this time. Like other succulents, place it outside in a sunny location and gradually increase the amount of water. For this arrangement that has moss on the soil, water the moss with a spray bottle. Touch the soil with your fingers and check its dryness before watering.

OCTOBER | C. Expressing the Unique Charm of the Season

Materials for this group planting

Layout

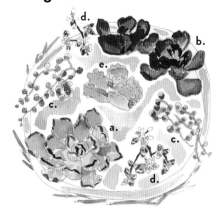

Plants

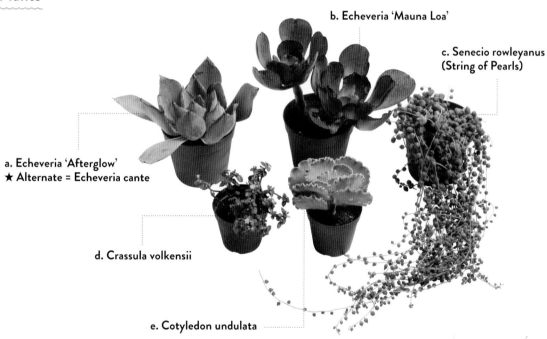

b. Echeveria 'Mauna Loa'

c. Senecio rowleyanus
(String of Pearls)

a. Echeveria 'Afterglow'
★ Alternate = Echeveria cante

d. Crassula volkensii

e. Cotyledon undulata

Pot

Ceramic pot:
Diameter 7" (180mm) x Height 4.75" (120mm)
Grapevine:
27–28" (700mm) x approx. 30 vines

How to Plant

1. Divide the Rowleyanus into two and plant a segment on the left, with its stems cascading over the edge.

2. Plant the Undulata inside 1. Because the seedling is short, plant it vertically to the soil.

3. Plant 'Afterglow' at the front left of the pot. Tilt the seedling forward.

4. Divide the Volkensii into two plants. Guide the stem of one segment to the front and center of the pot.

5. Plant the remaining Rowleyanus in front right of the pot with the stems cascading outward.

6. Plant 'Mauna Loa' in the back right.

7. Pin the center back plant the remaining Volkensii.

8. Loop the grapevine larger than the pot to create a ring.

9. Stack three loops and fit them onto the pot.

Finished

Tip: Styling with long stems.

When setting the vine in the pot, gather the hanging String of Pearls stems on top of the plants. Once the vines are set, take the stems down, a few at a time, loosely curl them up and style them. Hook them into the leaves of the Echeveria to create a vibrant, artistic group planting.

A bouquet-like arrangement made with succulents

One day, I happened upon a charming bouquet in a city flower shop. That became the impetus for my succulent potted arrangement creations.

Succulents that are perfect for bouquets

About a dozen years ago, when I was trying various plants and experimenting with arrangements, I happened upon a small bouquet in a florist shop. And I thought, "Why not make a bouquet-like arrangement using succulents?" The next day, I started creating arrangements with succulents. The beautiful leaves of Echeveria were reminiscent of roses, and the cascading form of String of Pearls reminded me of jasmine or ivy. That was the beginning of my journey into creating succulent bouquets.

However, having a good design isn't enough. These aren't cut flowers—you need to maintain them to keep them alive and well. There were failures, such as elongating the plants indoors or leaving them in the summer rain, and the plants melting in the heat and poor ventilation the next day. I still make mistakes, but every time new seedlings arrive, I get excited thinking about what kind of work I'll create tomorrow.

The above picture is from the book *365 Days of Yosegae Style (Spring/ Summer Season)*.

NOVEMBER

Realistic Dioramas Create New Worlds and Start Your Own Adventure!

My aim in this chilly month was to use succulents to create fresh landscapes. It's fun to put plants and minature items together to imitate different kinds of scenery.

A. Creating a Landscape with a Balance of Seedlings and Accessories

Idyllic succulent farm with small seedlings as vegetables

In a diorama-style potted arrangement, each seedling becomes a part of the landscape. I want to show the shape of the grass and leaves properly, so I don't plant them too closely, but instead place them while utilizing the space. With each plant, take a step back and create while balancing the whole.

In an antique wooden box, I placed a country-style hut and depicted a peaceful farm landscape by seeing succulents as vegetables. The main plant, *Crassula ovata*, is selected by looking at the balance with the hut. Furthermore, small seedlings such as wild roses and white peonies are seen as cabbages, while *Sedum reflexum* 'Chameleon' and *Crassula pruinosa* are seen as corn. Selecting and planting seedlings with these thoughts in mind is also fun.

Main plant: Echeveria 'Peach Pride' and Purpusorum, Crassula ovata
Supporting plant: Sedum sarmentosum

Echeveria 'Peach Pride' and *Purpusorum*, which resemble vegetables, are planted after mounding the soil like ridges of a field to bring out realism. Little sticks forming a trellis are placed by *Crassula pruinosa* and *Sedum Reflexum* 'Chameleon' to enhance the veggie garden effect.

B. Create a Three-Dimensional Image

A forest of succulents with depth and mystery, much like a painting

I used an antique picture frame as a canvas. With horizontally placed wood and moss added as a finishing touch, I've depicted a deep forest where ancient, giant trees thrive. For seedlings, I used those with unique colors like red, blue, yellow, and pastel green and those with distinctive leaf shapes to evoke a forest reminiscent of *Alice in Wonderland*.

Main plant: Kalanchoe behalensis
Supporting plant: Kalanchoe behalensis

This forest was planted in a wooden box attached to a picture frame. To make it look like an illustration, I avoided using taller grasses.

116

Dry savanna scene enhanced with fine Akadama soil

The large trees, dry soil, and plants living in
a harsh environment—succulents are great for
representing the scenery of the African savanna.
The seedlings were chosen to match the size
of the animal figures. To create a realistic
look, the trick is to place large seedlings in the
foreground to create a sense of perspective. The
soil around the large tree planted in the back is
higher toward the center and lower at the sides,
creating a gentle slope.

Main plant: Bowiea volubilis
Supporting plant: Haworthia fasciatai

Keep the Haworthia indoors in
full sun and drastically reduce
watering beginning in December.
Bowiea also should be watered
less in spring, when the vines
die and go into dormancy.
Otherwise, mist lightly every
2-3 weeks.

| # A. Creating a Landscape with a Balance of Seedlings and Accessories

Materials for this group planting

Layout

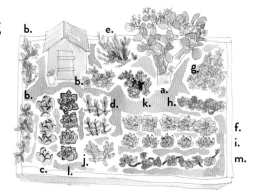

Plants

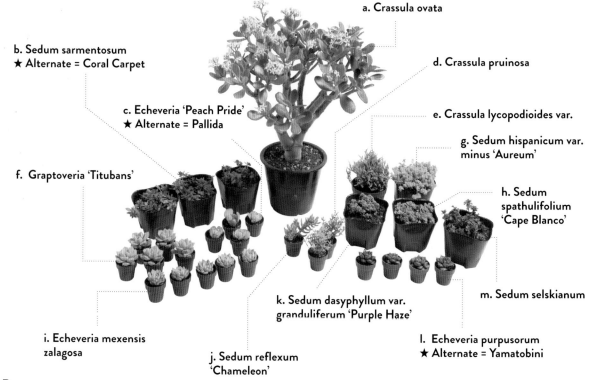

a. Crassula ovata

b. Sedum sarmentosum
★ Alternate = Coral Carpet

d. Crassula pruinosa

c. Echeveria 'Peach Pride'
★ Alternate = Pallida

e. Crassula lycopodioides var.

g. Sedum hispanicum var.
minus 'Aureum'

f. Graptoveria 'Titubans'

h. Sedum
spathulifolium
'Cape Blanco'

k. Sedum dasyphyllum var.
granuliferum 'Purple Haze'

m. Sedum selskianum

i. Echeveria mexensis
zalagosa

j. Sedum reflexum
'Chameleon'

l. Echeveria purpusorum
★ Alternate = Yamatobini

Pot

Wooden box:
Width 19.75" (500mm) x Depth 12.25" (310mm) x
Height 11" (280mm)
Miniature shed:
Width 4.75" (120mm) x Depth 5.25" (130mm) x
Height 5.25" (130mm)
Twigs/sticks (5.25" (130mm) x 7 twigs) /
Miscellaneous miniatures (buckets, wheelbarrows,
etc.) / Stones / Humus

How to Plant

1 First, determine the location of the hut and Ovata. The hut is placed at the far left.

2 Plant Ovata at the far right. The hut and Ovata will form the framework of the landscape.

3 Divide the roots of the two Sarmentosum and Lycopodioides v. plants in half, spread the plants out long and thin.

4 Plant the thinned and elongated Lycopodioides v. along the edge of the back side to form a hedge. Plant 'Aureum' at the back right.

5 Plant 'Cape Blanco' at the base of the Ovatum plant.

6 Plant 'Purple Haze' and Sarmentosum to the right of the shed.

7 Plant the remaining Sarmentosum, along the left side edge to make a hedge.

8 Plant Selskianum in small sections in the front right. Make ridges in the space in front.

9 Plant 'Peach Pride' on the ridges. taking care to space them evenly.

10 Similarly, plant Purpusorum, Pruinosa, Mexensisalagosa, and the Titubans.

11 In front of the hut, arrange stones to make a path.

12 Insert 3 thin sticks or twigs on both sides of the Pruinosa and 'Chameleon' rows to form a trellis.

(13) When you have finished inserting the sticks, pass the cross twigs/sticks and secure them with string or fine wire.

(14) Lightly sprinkle humus where soil is visible.

(15) Finish by placing your miniatures.

Finished

Tip: Making Sedum look like a hedge.

Instead of dividing the Sedum plant, hold the base of the plant with both hands, and divide the roots by about half. From there, spread it out and extend it in a straight line.

Miniature items like carts and buckets and so on help create a realistic scene.

Materials for this group planting

Layout

Plants

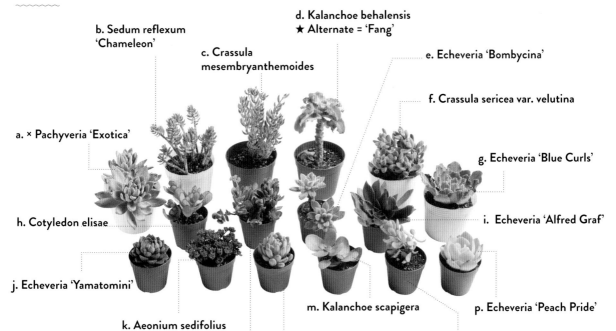

a. × Pachyveria 'Exotica'

b. Sedum reflexum 'Chameleon'

c. Crassula mesembryanthemoides

d. Kalanchoe behalensis ★ Alternate = 'Fang'

e. Echeveria 'Bombycina'

f. Crassula sericea var. velutina

g. Echeveria 'Blue Curls'

h. Cotyledon elisae

i. Echeveria 'Alfred Graf'

j. Echeveria 'Yamatomini'

k. Aeonium sedifolius

l. Crassula atropurpurea var. watermeyeri

m. Kalanchoe scapigera

n. Pachyphytum hookeri ★ Alternate= oviferum 'Azumabijin'

o. Cotyledon 'Tinkerbell'

p. Echeveria 'Peach Pride'

Pot

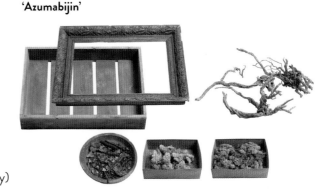

Antique picture frame:
Width 26.75" (680mm) x Depth 21" (530mm) x Height 5" (135mm)
Planting box:
Width 19.75" (500mm) x Depth 13.75" (350mm) x Height 4" (100mm)
Tree roots -3 / Humus / Moss (1 light and 1 dark variety)

How to Plant

1. Place the frame on the planting box and insert a pot bottom mesh.

2. Fill the box eighty percent full with soil.

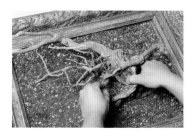

3. Arrange the tree roots in the center, burying the bottom part in the soil to secure.

4. Plant the central back area. Plant the 'Blue Curl's between the branches and soil, tilting it forward.

5. Plant 'Bombycina' at the back left of 4.

6. Plant on the left side. Put the tallest 'Chameleon' at the far left.

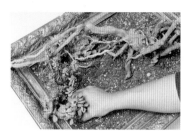

7. Divide the Velutina in a 2:1 ratio and plant the larger portion in front of 6.

8. Plant 'Alfred Graf' at the front left.

9. Plant 'Tinkerbell' to the right of 'Alfred Graf'.

10. In front of 9, on the right, plant 'Yamatomini'.

11. Plant Scapigera between 'Alfred Graf' and 'Yamatomini', completing the left portion.

12. For the right back section, plant Mesembryanthemoides beside the branches.

13 Plant 'Exotica' in the right back, arranging smaller plants along the edge.

14 To the right of the Mesembryanthemoides, plant the rest of the divided Velutina.

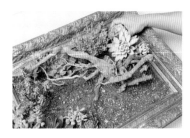

15 Plant 'Peach Pride' in the far right corner.

16 Plant the front right section. Plant Behalensis, the tallest plant in this section.

17 Plant Watermeyeri to the right of Behalensis, directing the stem outward to give a sense of spread.

18 Divide Sedifolius into two and plant a segment in front left of Behalensis.

19 Plant the remaining Sedifolius under the center branch.

20 Plant Elisae in front of Sedifolius to the right.

21 Plant Hookeri in front of Elisae.

22 The seedlings are now planted.

23 Cover the exposed soil with moss. Use dark green moss on the right side of the branch.

24 Cover the left side with light green moss, hiding the soil.

(25) Lightly sprinkle humus on top of the moss to represent the forest floor.

(26) Decorate the roots of the second tree.

(27) Decorate the roots of the final tree to finish.

Finished

Tip: Plant one area at a time.

First, decide on the arrangement of the three roots. Use the curve of the roots to draw an arch and create a three-dimensional atmosphere around the base of the giant tree. As the area to be planted is wide, divide it into four areas: center back, right back, left, and right front. Choose species with different heights, sizes, and colors and plant them with variations in height in each area.

NOVEMBER | C. Perspective Creates a Sense of Vastness

Materials for this group planting

Layout

Plants

a. Bowiea volubilis

b. Haworthia fasciata

c. Haworthia truncata 'Lime Green'

d. Crassula atropurpurea var. watermeyeri

e. Crassula expansa spp. fragilis

f. Adromischus cooperi 'Tenkinshou'

g. Villadia batesii

h. Haworthia cymbiformis var. umbraticola

i. Crassula remota

j. Haworthia parva

k. Haworthia turgida var. turgida

l. Crassula 'Tom Thumb'

m. Haworthia turgida cv.

n. Echeveria 'Iria'

Pot

Tinplate box:
Width 22.75" (580mm) x Depth 16.5" (420mm) x
Height 4" (105mm)
Animal figures / Tree branches /
Miniature car / Moss / Akadama soil (fine grain)

How to Plant

1. Place the tree root in the center back of the pot and fill the pot eighty percent full with soil.

2. The soil should be slightly higher in the center and lower around the rim of the vessel.

3. Plant Bowiea to the left of the tree root and wrap its vines around the tree.

4. Plant a large Fasciata front and left of the tree. The seedling should be perpendicular to the soil.

5. Plant a smaller Fasciata in the center, with the seedlings perpendicular to the soil, as in 4.

6. Plant the 'Tenkinshou' in the center front.

7. Plant 'Lime Green' in the right front corner.

8. Plant Watermeyeri in the back right. Tilt the seedlings slightly forward to the left.

9. Plant Umbraticola at the far right of 'Tenkinshou'. Tilt the seedlings slightly forward.

10. Plant Turgida cv. in front of Umbraticola to the left.

11. Plant var. Turgida in the front left corner.

12. Plant Parva to the left of 'Tenkinshou'.

(13) Plant Batesii at the base of the stump in front of the tree.

(14) Plant 'Iria' at the front right of Fasciata.

(15) Divide 'Tom Thumb' into two and plant one segment at the base of the tree.

(16) Plant the remaining 'Tom Thumb' in front of Fasciata.

(17) Plant Remota at the right end of Umbraticola.

(18) Plant Fragilis at the back right and front right.

(19) Plant the remaining Fragilis in the back left corner.

(20) Randomly place moss at the base of plants.

(21) Sprinkle Akadama soil to create the look of a dry biome.

Finished

Tip: Enhance the atmosphere with the tree root and Bowiea volubilis vines.

Use dried tree roots placed upside down as large trees. For a spacious landscape appearance, place them towards the back. The Bowiea volubilis vines cannot stand by themselves, so intertwine them with the tree roots. Once you've created a dry safari atmosphere with Akadama soil, finish the arrangement it by placing animal figures.

DECEMBER

Welcome Christmas with a Container Garden Full of Life and Hope

As December begins, the town is all about Christmas. Streets are full of light, colorful decorations abound. Decorate your own space in a Christmas spirit. Make it colorful with red and green succulents or luxurious with pink and white ones. Finish it off with festive ornaments for an arrangement that cheers the heart.

A. An Easy and Versatile Group Planting

An elegant and festive Christmas tree-style creation

Succulents are perfect for Christmas arrangements. If you choose Christmas colors like red and green, it'll be a glamorous arrangement. Using light-colored succulents like the silver ones will create an elegant pot that reminds you of a white Christmas. Instead of a flower arrangement for this year's Christmas party, why not decorate with a succulent arrangement?

Display succulents planted in clear glass pots like a champagne tower. By combining varieties in reddish-purple such as *Graptoveria* 'Debbie' and *Echeveria Shaviana* 'Pink Frills' with silver-colored succulents like the Kalanchoe varieties we used here, you can easily evoke the Christmas atmosphere. If you remove the Santa Claus and other seasonal decorations, you can continue to enjoy this festively elegant arrangement.

Main plant: Echeveria Shaviana 'Pink Frills', Graptoveria 'Debbie'
Supporting plant: Graptoveria 'Titubans', Kalanchoe eriophylla

Keep in a sunny location indoors, changing the location of the container every few days or rotating the racks so that all succulents get equal exposure to the sun. Water the succulents once every 2 to 3 weeks with a misting spray.

B. Arrange Colorfully, as if Painting a Picture

Colorful tapestry-like arrangement in Christmas colors

The vessels used were Christmas-themed baking pans and molds. Placing them on a table and adding a candle enhances the Christmas mood. The planting procedure is the same for both the tree and the star: while observing the color balance, scatter the main seedlings and fill the empty spaces with divided Sedum. Do not plant too densely, lay moss between the plants. Enjoy coloring as if you were painting a picture.

Main plant: Christmas tree & large star: Graptosedum 'Francesco Baldi' / Small star: Sedum 'Alice Evans'
Supporting plant: Christmas tree: Echeveria 'Mebina' Echeveria 'Mebina'
Large star: Crassula schmidtii / Small star: Crassula excilis ssp. 'Cooperi'

C. Enhancing the Allure of Mystical Foliage Colors

Christmas wreath reminiscent of the holy night.

This wreath conjures the image of a calm Christmas night filled with silvery light. The main plant is a silver-colored Echeveria that looks like a fully bloomed rose. To avoid a flat impression, I planted clusters of baby plants and larger plants alternately. This wreath is beautiful all winter, just as it is. It's also lovely to decorate with Christmas-y items like pinecones, cinnamon sticks, walnuts, and dried fruits.

Main plant: Echeveria subsessilis, Echeveria lilacina
Supporting plant: Echeveria 'Iria', Echeveria, 'Ginbugen'

Spanish moss covers the topsoil and hides the soil between the plants. Its gray color coordinates beautifully with the tones of the Echeveria.

DECEMBER | A. An Easy and Versatile Group Planting

Materials for this group planting

Layout

Plants

a. × Graptoveria 'Debbie'
★ Alternate = 'First Love'

b. Cotyledon undulate

c. Kalanchoe tomentosa 'Ginger'

d. Crassula pruinosa

e. Kalanchoe eriophylla
★ Alternate = Kalanchoe tomentosa (Panda plant)

f. Kalanchoe pumila

g. Senecio rowleyanus

n. Kalanchoe tomentosa
f. nigromarginatas

h. × Graptoveria 'Titubans'
★ Alternate = 'Lovely Rose'

k. Echeveria Shaviana 'Pink Frills'
★ Alternate = 'Takasago no Okina'

i. Pachyphytum oviferum 'Tsukibijin'

m. Tillandsia usneoide

l. Othonna capensis

j. Echeveria subsessilis

Pot

Three-tier rack:
Diameter 13" (330mm) x Height 27" (690mm)
Glass Pot:
Diameter 2.5" (65mm) x Height 3" (80mm) 12 pieces
Culture soil for succulent plants / Root
rot inhibitor

How to Plant

Finished

(1) After adding root rot inhibitor, fill half way with soil, plant the seedlings and add more soil.

(2) Poke the soil with a thin stick to settle it. Then simply arrange the potted plants as per the layout illustration on page 132.

Tip 1: Use the stick to acclimate the soil in the pot.

After taking the seedling out of its pot, gently loosen the roots and plant. After adding the soil, use a thin stick to make sure the soil goes in deeply. For plants like Graptoveria 'Debbie' that overhang the edge of the pot, lift the leaves gently with your fingers, add soil, and then poke with the stick.

Tip 2: Select soil that looks good and drains well.

Since the arrangement is viewed from the side, you'll want to be choosy about the soil inside the pot. Rather than using general-purpose cultivation soil, it's recommended to use a visually appealing soil with superior drainage for succulents and put a root rot prevention agent at the bottom. You can also mix small-grain pumice (5), vermiculite (2), akadama soil (2), and activated charcoal (1).

Tip 3: Choose varieties that remind you of a tree in the snow.

Use shabby three-tiered racks to resemble a Christmas tree to create a white Christmas image, with Othonna capensis and Senecio rowleyanus in green to create a fir tree hue, red and purple 'Pink Frills' and 'Debbie' as ornaments, and the silvery varieties as fallen snow.

DECEMBER | B. Arrange Colorfully, as if Painting a Picture

Materials for this group planting

Layout

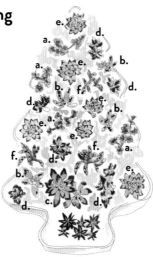

Plants (Tree)

a. Sedum selskianum

b. Kalanchoe tomentosa 'Golden Girl'

c. Echeveria harmsii
★ Alternate = 'Ginkousei'

d. Sinocrassula indica

e. Echeveria 'Mebina'
★ Alternate = 'Harry Butterfield'

f. Crassula excilis ssp. 'Cooperi'

Pot

Christmas tree shaped candy baking pot:
Width 9.75" (245mm) x Depth 13.5" (345mm) x
Height 2" (50mm)
Moss / Star anise / Humus

How to Plant (Tree)

1 Fill the pot to about eighty percent full with soil and plant the Harmsii at the most noticeable point

2 Divide the 'Mebina' into individual plants and scatter them throughout.

3 Similarly, divide the 'Golden Girl' into individual plants and scatter throughout.

4 For the standout Indica, divide one plant into three and distribute evenly.

5 Divide the Cooperi plants and plant them at the base of the Harmsii and 'Golden Girl' plants.

6 Divide Selskianum into 5-6 plants. Plant in a way that covers the spaces between the plants.

7 Add moss to the parts where soil is visible to hide it.

8 Spread humus at the base of the tree where no plants were planted.

9 Place Star Anise over the humus to finish.

Finished

Tip: Even bottomless vessels can be transformed into pots with some ingenuity!

For tree-shaped containers with a base, we drilled holes for drainage. However, for star-shaped containers without a base, we attached a mesh at the bottom using wires. We drilled holes 5-6mm from the edge of the base of the star shape. We passed the wire through the holes and attached a mesh that we cut to fit the star shape.

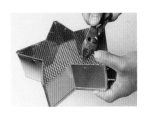

Layout

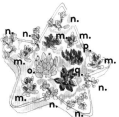

Plants

(Star • Large)

(Star • Small)

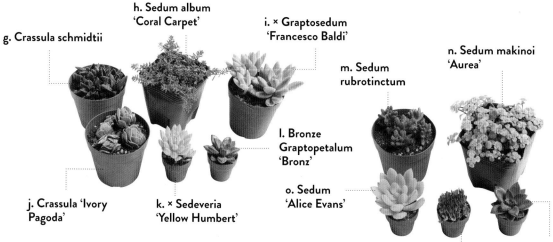

g. Crassula schmidtii

h. Sedum album 'Coral Carpet'

i. × Graptosedum 'Francesco Baldi'

j. Crassula 'Ivory Pagoda'

k. × Sedeveria 'Yellow Humbert'

l. Bronze Graptopetalum 'Bronz'

m. Sedum rubrotinctum

n. Sedum makinoi 'Aurea'

o. Sedum 'Alice Evans'

p. Orostachys japonica ★ Alternate = Crassida pellucida

q. Bronz Graptopetalum 'Bronz'

Pot

Baking tin:
Large star: Diameter 8" (200mm) x Height 2.75" (70mm)
Small star: Diameter 5.75" (145mm) x Height 2" (55mm)

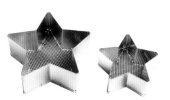

Complete

How to Plant (Star • Big)

1 Plant 'Francesco Baldi' in the center and surround it with 'Yellow Humbert', 'Bronz', and 'Ivory Pagoda'.

2 Plant Schmidtii to surround the center plants and fill in the gaps with 'Coral Carpet'.

For the small star, follow the layout illustration using plants **m.** through **q.**

DECEMBER | C. Enhancing the Allure of Mystical Foliage Colors

Materials for this group planting

Layout

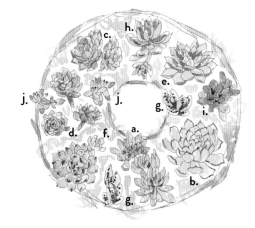

Plants

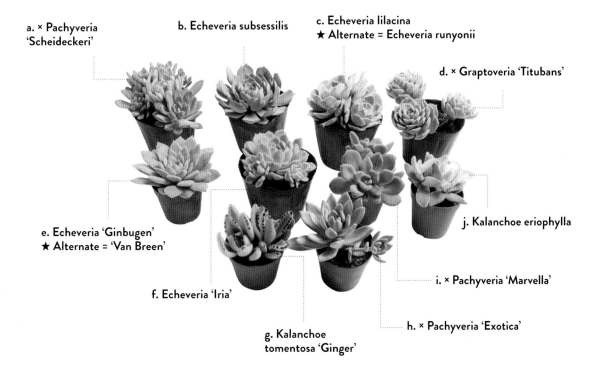

a. × Pachyveria 'Scheideckeri'

b. Echeveria subsessilis

c. Echeveria lilacina
★ Alternate = Echeveria runyonii

d. × Graptoveria 'Titubans'

e. Echeveria 'Ginbugen'
★ Alternate = 'Van Breen'

f. Echeveria 'Iria'

g. Kalanchoe tomentosa 'Ginger'

h. × Pachyveria 'Exotica'

i. × Pachyveria 'Marvella'

j. Kalanchoe eriophylla

Pot

Wicker wreath form:
Diameter 13.75" (350mm) x Height 4.25" (110mm)
Spanish moss

How to Plant

(1) Fill the wreath form to eighty percent capacity the soil and plant the Lilacina and 'Titubans'.

(2) Plant Eriophylla in the space between the 'Titubans' plants.

(3) In front of the 'Titubans', plant the pale green 'Iria' to add variety.

(4) Divide the 'Ginger' into two and plant one on the outer edge in front of the 'Iria'.

(5) Inside of the area from step 4, plant 'Scheideckeri' in a manner that embeds it. Position them to create a difference in height.

(6) To the right of 'Scheideckeri', plant Subsessilis and to its right, plant Oviferum closer to the outer edge.

(7) Inside of Oviferum, plant the remaining divided 'Ginger'.

(8) Behind the area from step 6, plant 'Ginbugen', and between the initially planted Lilacina and 'Ginbugen' plant 'Exotica'.

(9) In the spaces where the soil is exposed, garnish with small amounts of Spanish moss.

Finished

> **Tip: Create a three-dimensional effect by varying size and color.**
>
> Place 'Iria', Subsessilis, 'Ginbugen', etc., next to large plants, and place 'Titubans' and 'Oviferum' next to them, adding contrast in color and size. In the case of a wreath, an extreme difference in height is not necessary, but by utilizing the height of each plant and creating some level of height difference when planting, you can create a natural texture.

Basics 1 to 6

Basics of Succulent Planting and Care

This section introduces some basics you should know for succulent planting and care, plus tips for choosing the right seedlings. With this info, you'll be able to create and maintain beautiful succulent container gardens!

Basics 1: Tools You'll Need for Container Gardening

Make sure you have the essential tools

It's not necessary to have every tool introduced, but at the very least, scissors and a watering can are essentials. Bamboo skewers, used to help roots and soil mesh together, can be substituted with items like disposable chopsticks. When handling sharp cacti, leather gloves can be handy.

Scissors
Used for trimming the arrangement or cutting unnecessary roots during replanting.

Soil scoop
A tool for adding soil when planting. It's very convenient to have these in different sizes.

Bamboo skewers
Useful during planting in small pots, especially when it's hard to fill soil between the pot and the plant.

Gloves
Used when handling prickly plants like cacti or Euphorbia during replanting or arranging.

Spray bottle/mister
Supplies moisture to the soil surface. Useful during dormant periods or when planting in containers without holes.

Watering Can
For arrangements and small pots, a narrow-spouted watering can is more practical.

Basics 2: Types of Pots to Use

Select according to the atmosphere of the arrangement you want to create.

If you get the trick of watering, you can use just about any container

Pots with drainage holes are ideal for watering as excess water gets expelled through the holes. These also ensure a good flow of oxygen in the soil, making them suitable for cultivating succulent plants. There are various materials to choose from, but for beginners, clay pots that evaporate water efficiently are best. If you use containers without drainage holes, it's important to carefully observe how much water you provide and how many days it takes for the soil to dry, to establish a proper watering rhythm.

Gardening pots

Available at gardening stores or home centers. They come in various materials like clay, ceramic, plastic, metal, or wicker baskets. Functional and easy to use, especially for beginners

Resin pots

Wicker wreath forms

Omoto pots

Bonsai pots

Ceramic pots

Everyday items

Many of these can't have drainage holes, so it's crucial to use well-draining soil, add more stones at the bottom, use rot-prevention additives, and adjust the water quantity and frequency.

Ceramic bowl

Glass bowl

Wok

Antiques and other miscellaneous items

Once you're more familiar with cultivating succulent plants, trying out antique or unique containers is a good idea, especially if you want to add originality or a sense of depth.

Antique pots

Wooden barrels

Baking tins

Glass cases

Brass weighing scales

Baking molds

Metal planters

DIY + Creative ideas

Incorporate unique items like a frame combined with a handmade wooden box or attaching a mesh at the bottom of a baking mold. With some creativity, items that don't typically serve as pots can transform into unique plant holders.

Basics 3: About the Soil to Use
Choose the right soil to grow healthy succulent plants.

Improving drainage in the pot and avoiding excessive moisture is key.

Pots with drainage holes are ideal as excess water gets expelled during watering, ensuring a good flow of oxygen in the soil. For those new to growing succulents, clay pots that allow effective evaporation of water are recommended. When using containers without holes, monitor the soil drying time after watering to establish a rhythm.

When I make succulent arrangements, I often use soil meant for flowers, but I might add akadama soil for better drainage. There are also soils specifically for succulents and cacti available. These might be perlite-based or akadama-based. For smaller pots or compact arrangements that require high drainage, perlite-based soils are recommended. For beginners, akadama-based soils, which let you easily check the soil's moisture level, are suitable.

Regardless of the soil mix, good drainage is essential. Place stones or large grains of akadama at the bottom of the pots for this purpose.

Root rot inhibitor
When using a container without a drainage hole, place pottings stones/pebbles first, then add this. It also promotes rooting.

Potting soil
Normally, use a culture medium for flowers and plants. To improve drainage, mix red-bean soil or add more potting stones.

Potting stones/pebbles
To improve drainage, these are placed at the bottom of the pot. Use one-fifth of the pot's volume, and for larger pots, use two-fifths.

Akadama-soil–small grain
When using culture medium for flowers, mix 20-30% akadama soil to improve drainage.

Succulents/ Cactus soil
There are types that prioritize drainage with small-grained pumice base, and others close to the akadama base for flowering plants.

Akadama soil
Large-grain Akadama-soil is used as potting stones—heavier than commercially available potting stones, but less expensive.

Basics 4: Mixing your own soil

Mixing soil to control the growth of group plantings.

Original soils for different purposes

Depending on the style of your arrangement and the size of the pot, there will be plants that you want to grow large and others you'll want to keep compact. You can control this by fertilizing, pruning, etc., but the growth conditions will also vary depending on the base soil mix.

To grow large or promote fast growth, use akadama-based soil for succulents or soil for flowering plants. To improve the drainage of the flowering plant's soil, mix in 20-30% small grains of akadama. The larger the soil grains, the better the drainage. When making your own soil mix, adjust the materials and proportions according to the purpose.

A. Compact, well-drained mix

Make it 50% pumice, emphasizing drainage. It lacks fertility, so fertilizers are necessary. Use liquid fertilizer, not solid.

* Pumice, small grains   5
* Vermiculite   2
* Akadama soil, small grains   2
* Rice husk charcoal   1

B. For larger growth, a moisture-retaining mix

This is a formula that promotes growth by emphasizing fertilizer retention, water retention, and aeration. Pumice stone is used to improve drainage and rice husk charcoal to prevent root rot. Both solid and liquid fertilizers can be used.

* Akadama soil, small grains   4
* Humus   2
* Pumice stone, small grains   2
* Vermiculite   1
* Rice husk charcoal   1

Basics 5: Things to keep in mind before group planting

Seedling selection and planting techniques that prolong the life of group plantings.

A. Choosing seedlings for group planting

It is difficult to imagine the shape, size, and speed of growth of seedlings when they are in their seedling state. It is advisable to check the characteristics of the plants in advance and avoid combining plants with extremely different characteristics. There are two types of succulents: summer-type succulents that grow from spring to fall and winter-type succulents that grow from fall to winter, but group planting is possible even if they do not share the same growth type. If growing plants disturb dormant ones, prune them.

B. Notes and precautions

For succulents, even if you remove a lot of the root ball, they won't die. However, removing too much can destabilize the plant, making it hard to plant. The soil of the root ball is easier to plant and more stable when you trim its sides and leave it elongated. After planting, pressing the soil too hard can crush its granular structure, worsening drainage. Moreover, if the stem or leaves get buried, the seedling might rot, so avoid adding too much soil.

Basics 6: Recommended varieties for different purposes

Each characteristic is a factor in choosing your plants. Here, we help you choose according to your needs.

A. Plants that are perfect for the leading role

Plants with characteristic foliage color, seedling size, shape, and form that make them suitable for the main character of the group planting.

Campfire
In winter, the leaves turn bright red, contrasting nicely with yellow-green and green plants. p.6

Francesco Baldi
Goes well with chic reddish-brown or deep red leaf varieties. p.9

Bronze
Turns a chic reddish-brown in winter. Interesting when you keep its natural shape without pruning. p.9

Harry Butterfield
Bright leaf color is beautiful. If using low in a wreath form, pruning is necessary. p.38

Cooperi
Dislikes strong summer sunlight. Pair with Haworthia and Gasteria, best for indoors. p.53

Topsy Turvy
Placing it in the front makes the piece more impressive. Goes well with purple or pink foliage. p.52

Lophantha var.
A small Agave. It has a similar leaf shape to Aloe, easy to coordinate. p.72

Domingo
Pale blue foliage contrasts well with darker foliage. p.94

Lilacina
Use its elegant impression as the lead in a gorgeous pot planting. p.131

Subsessilis
When used as the main plant, goes well with pink. The leaf tips turn pink in winter. p.131

B. Plants that highlight the leading role

Varieties that shine by highlighting the main plants, serving a highly convenient and important role.

Watermeyeri
Grows stems sideways and upwards, valuable as a supporting role. Beautiful fall to spring colors. p.19

Golden Glow
A tilting appearance makes pot planting three-dimensional. Bright yellow-green leaves are vibrant. p.18

Tomentosa
Matches well with blue, green, and other pastel-colored plants. p.74

Conjuncta
Can be displayed in many ways; effective when placed next to the main plant, contrasting the shape and form of the leaves. p.52

Paraguayense
A hardy species that can withstand temperatures as low as 32°F /0°C. It adds movement and dynamism to group plantings. p.52

Mesembryanthemoides
When paired with short plants, creates height differences, making it three-dimensional. p.75

Frosty
Beautiful silver leaves, gives a cool impression in summer pot planting. p.103

Velutina
Useful when you want to plant it to droop or add volume. p.116

Tinkerbell
Grows upwards without taking up space, recommended when you want to add color. p.116

Golden Girl
Leaves covered in white hairs, ideal for adding warmth, perfect supporting role for winter pot planting. p.130

C. Plants with height to use at the back or center

When adding height to an arrangement, consider whether your taller plants should be in the back or the center. Decide which placement creates the necessary balance, and plant accordingly.

Copper Spoons
Pair with silver or deep green leaves for a lovely color balance. p.8

Undulatum
The leaf tips turn slightly red in winter. Works best when planted in the center. p.18

Sunburst
Aeonium with beautiful mottled leaves. Pair with shorter plants. p.41

Fang
A beautiful, neat-looking plant, best used to display the base of the plant. p.41

Danguyi
Stretches its vines neatly upwards. Interesting to use at the very back or center. p.75

var. Pseudolycopodi
Grows upward. Utilize its height or to create movement in the middle. p.75

Yoshitsune no Mai
It gives a chic impression. Grows upward while branching. A good complementary plant. p.75

Mikado
Stylish with narrow, straight leaves. Ideal for indoor group planting. p.82

Dichtoma
This plant has an imposing form and should be paired with shorter plants. p. 92

Cashmere Violet
The new leaves in the center are a deep green. Useful in both main and supporting roles. p. 95

D. Plants with large leaves as a point of interest

Characteristic for their large leaves, they're easy to use in large pots for arrangements, and valuable as featured plants.

Queen Red
Large red leaves can be enjoyed year-round. Perfect for planter-type arrangements. p.18

Kakurei
Grows tall, ideal for the main or highlight use in large pot arrangements. p.18

Orbiculata
Distinctive leaves make a statement in arrangements. Can also give a refreshing impression. p.50

Pallida
The upright flower stalks accentuate large group plantings. p.95

Red Baron
Not suitable for small pot arrangements. Use dynamically in large pot arrangements. p.95

Early Light
A large Echeveria, make it the star for a unique arrangement. p.94

Princess Pearl
Pairing with white or silver plants will make a strong statement. p.94

Mauna Loa
The leaves turn bright red in winter and go well with blue-gray and silver plants. p.105

Afterglow
A large Echeveria species. Enjoy the beautiful leaf colors with a few plants. p.105

Behalensis
Felt-like leaves covered with fine hairs. It grows gradually in height. p.116

E. Plants with charming small leaves

The endearing form significantly impacts the overall pot arrangement and plays a vital role in bringing it all together.

Rubens
It looks elegant when planted in a way that it grows upright, then cascades over the edge of a pot. (p.31)

Chameleon
Blue-tinted foliage, invaluable for filling gaps and adding movement. (p.74)

Little Gem
Compact, spreading, creeping plant. Charming when overhanging the pot's edge. p.50

Batesii
It produces many fine dark green leaves and is often used to fill in the space between plants. p.50

Tenjiku
Slow-growing, ideal for diorama-type or tapestry gardens. p.85

Tom Thumb
The tips of the leaves are slightly reddish. Useful for adding freshness. p.85

Volkensii
Grows horizontally. It can be used to fill in gaps by nestling it next to the main or supporting plants. p.105

Pruinosa
Grows branches upward. Cut back for a lower landscape. p.104

Fragilis
Nice for mixing with other horizontally-growing annuals. p.117

Sedifolius
The reddish-brown pattern is unique. Interesting to use as an accent. p.116

F. Plants with deep colors to use as accents

Their beautiful dark leaf color is essential for color coordination. Learning to use them skillfully is a pleasant challenge.

Indica
Green leaves from spring to summer, deep red leaves from fall to winter. For group planting in small pots. p.9

Opal
A chic dark reddish brown from fall to late spring. For when you want to have a crisp, clean look. p.52

Perle von Nuremberg
Purple all year round, but it becomes darker and more beautiful in winter. Easy to use as a main plant. p.40

Prostatum
Dark brown all year round. It complements aloe and other plants. p.92

Black Prince
A dark brown with blackish tints, recommended as a mainstay in chic group plantings. p.95

Alfred Graf
Similar to Black Prince, this brown foliage is ideal for color coordination. Use at the base of taller plants. p. 116

Yamatomini
The reddish-brown edges are beautiful. Use as a mainstay or point of interest for chic arrangements. p. 116

Mebina
Its leaves are light green in summer and the tips turn red in fall and spring. Can overwinter outside in warm climates. p.130

Pink Frills
Pink to purple leaves with small frilled edges. Can be used as a mainstay among plants in the same color scheme. p.128

Debbie
White powdery leaves which turn a deep pink in winter. Use as a focal point. p.128

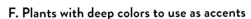

G. Plants that create a gentle impression with light colors

When creating a gradation of shades or a feminine style.

Yellow Humbert
Branches and grows upward. It's easy to add movement and goes well with any type. p.18

Alice Evans
Grows in clusters. When placed next to darker colors, they complement each other. p.19

Millotii
Popular for its charming leaf color. Recommended for indoor arrangements during winter. p.19

Antandroi
When grown into a large plant, it exudes presence. It's interesting when used at the center. p.19

Prolifera
Extends its branches in all directions, and is used in a drooping manner. Be cautious, as leaves might come off easily. p.16

Van Breen
Its light green leaf color enhances the main plant. Pairs excellently with dark green colors. p.38

Treleasei
Grows upward; cut back as needed to keep height low. p. 38

Xantii
Impressive pale blue, thin, pointed leaves. Place next to darker colors. p.93

Mexensis zalagosa
The leaves are stacked to form a beautiful rosette. Ideal as a main plant. p.114

Titubans
Tolerant of cold, can be grown on a balcony or under eaves at temperatures down to 32°F (0°C). p.114

H. Plants with unique forms

Just one can exude a compelling presence, but they can also complement main plants.

Jade Necklace
Grows with a twisty stem. Using the wild type gives a unique appearance. p.19

Undulata
Leaves dusted in white powder with wavy tips. Its leaves are unique but easy to pair with others. p.74

Compactum
Firm leaves with a compact growth pattern. Suitable for small pot arrangements. p.38

Tenkinshou
Distinctive leaf shape and spots. This variety's leaves might come off easily, so handle with care. p.53

Trigynus
Grows in clusters but maintains a compact form. Effective when planted at the base of taller plants. p.75

Moon Glow
Unique growth with overlapping triangular leaves. Plant on the edge of a pot for added accent. p.75

Sunburst
The crested form has a distinctive shape. When used as a stand-in for a large tree, it's intriguing. p.85

Bella
Leaves spread radially. Pairing with upright types makes it look stylish. p.82

Lime Green
Combine with other Haworthias of different shapes and colors, such as round or mottled leaves. p.117

Ivory Pagoda
Silver leaves covered with short white hairs. For small group plantings. p.130

I. Plants with long stems to create nuance
Enhance style by using draping varieties in hanging pots.

Athorum
Cute silver leaves. Handy when you want to fill space. p.18

Herreanus
Grows extending its tendrils. Beautifully drapes, perfect for hanging types. p.16

David
Short internodes and low height make it suitable for group planting in wreaths and small pots. p.38

Woodii f. variegata
Popular for its pink, heart-shaped leaves. Combine with pastels. p.53

Rowleyanus variegata
A spotted Rowleyanus (String of Pearls) . It stands out when placed next to dark greens. p.82

Makinoi f. variegata
A beautifully mottled, sideways-crawling variegation. Pairs well with dark red or purple leaves. p.94

Ruby
A beautifully spaced, horizontal creeping plant that grows well with darker red and purple foliage. p.94

Rowleyanus
A must for bouquet style and works well with all succulents. p.105

Aureum
Roots emerge from the nodes of the vine. Vigorous grower, so prune often. p.114

Capencis
A member of the Othonna family. You can enjoy the gradations of green throughout the year. p.128

J. Plants with beautiful winter foliage that add color and vibrancy
Green-leafed varieties in spring and summer turn red in winter, offering more selection options.

Dragon's Blood
The chic reddish-brown leaves turn a bright deep red in the cold. A perfect accent. p.18

Tricolor
During winter, the pink leaves become redder due to the cold. Useful when you want to add color. p.31

Fusca
Turns vividly red s in winter. Contrasts beautifully with light green and yellow foliage. p.6

Aurora
Turns completely red in winter. Use separated clusters as an accent. p.9

Scapigera
Yellow-green leaves also turn bright red in winter. Pair with yellow or green leaves and manage indoors. p.116

K. Cacti easy to use for group planting
While cacti give a hard impression, you can enjoy mixing distinctive varieties.

Leninghausii
Easily obtainable and ideal as a main plant. Accentuates when paired with a dark green type. p.65

Geminispina
Has hook-like spines, so be careful when planting to avoid snagging. p.65

Plumosa
Use with tall columnar cacti to create height differences. p.64

Ritteri
Covered in long white hairs. Pairs well with similar colors and dark green types. p.64

Capilliformis
A thornless, epiphytic species that is easy to handle. Ensure good air circulation by thinning branches from the base. p.64

Basics 1 to 6

Master the Basic Techniques of Combining Succulents

For beautiful group plantings, the basics include color and texture coordination, balancing sizes and shapes, and a good placement of seedlings

Basics 1: Choose seedlings with different heights to create balance

Choose seedlings based on their height differences and become proficient in balance. For vibrant arrangements that you'd want to use as focal points in gardens or near windows:

Create group plantings with movement by varying the height of the seedlings themselves.

By emphasizing height differences and combining seedlings accordingly, vertical lines become more pronounced due to taller seedlings. This method can produce dynamism and vibrancy, making it perfect for spatial focal points. When planting, it's basic to place taller seedlings at the back, shorter ones at the front, and medium ones in between. Hanging drooping species in front of the pot creates a sense of unity between the plant and pot, introducing movement.

Type A: Combining two types of seedlings, tall and short

A simple style using tall and short seedlings. When the tall seedling is 1.5 to 2 times the height of the pot, the balance is good.

Type B: Combination of three types of seedlings: tall, medium, and short

Choose tall, medium, and short seedlings, and arrange them so that each plant's form is clearly visible. This is slightly more complex than type a, so it's good to decide on a rough arrangement before planting.

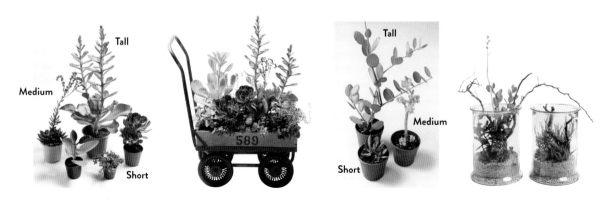

Basics 2: Mastering color coordination

Beautiful coordination maximizes the individuality of the leaves' colors.

Color coordination determines the arrangement's "flavor."

Succulent plants offer a rich palette of colors, including shades of red, green, silver, and even bluish tones. Especially during the winter season when they change color, you can enjoy contrasting arrangements. Multi-colored combinations give a lively, pop atmosphere. However, overdoing it may result in a chaotic look, which might be more suitable for experts. Arrangements with colors from the same family are foolproof, making it easy to coordinate. Complementary colors are those opposite each other on the color wheel. These combinations produce vibrant, contrasting impressions.

Type A: Coordinating with Multiple Colors

Coordinate a variety of colors with accents of darker or more vivid colors. Different colors are placed next to each other to enhance each other's hues.

Red plants
A large plant with splendid fall foliage is the star of the show. Place it in the center for maximum visibility

Green plants
These give complementary contrast to the red plants, enhancing their appearance.

Yellow plants
The contrast between red and green is softened by introducing yellow.

Silver plants
This color doesn't fit the conventional color wheel but serves as a highlight in the arrangement.

Type B: Coordinating with Gradient Shades of the Same Color

Unified coordination created with shades from pink to red. The plants are arranged to appear round and full from every angle.

Front

Left side

Right side

Back

Type C: Coordinating with Complementary Colors

Green **Red**

Red and green are complementary colors
Complementary colors are red and green, purple and yellow, and blue and orange. For succulents, the combination of red and green is easy to create.

Basics 3: Techniques to unify based on plant colors and features
Selecting the right plants to achieve a sophisticated arrangement.

Simple and easy-to-maintain group planting with unified characteristics and varieties.

By coordinating the colors, height, and types of the plants, you can enhance the completeness of the arrangement. For color coordination, decide on the color of the plants based on the theme and introduce variations in shade and leaf form for contrast. Using a slightly lighter or darker shade in an arrangement of similar hues creates a point of interest, avoiding a monotonous look. Arrangements of plants from the same family or with the same properties are easier to plan and maintain after planting. If you aim for a rounded arrangement, standardizing plant height makes planting easier and minimizes errors for beginners.

Type A: Unifying by leaf color

When aiming for uniformity with the same color, combine elements with completely different foliage shapes or subtle variations. A wreath unified in the pastel green palette exudes a refreshing atmosphere, giving the impression of spring's young leaves.

Type B: Unifying by plant type

To successfully unify by plant type, it's important to consider the needs and growth periods of the plants you wish to combine.

When unifying by plant type, it's easier to manage daily care since the light conditions and watering frequency will be consistent.

Type C: Unifying by plant height

It is easy to create a rounded, compact plant by matching the height of the seedlings. It is easier to create a rounded silhouette if the soil in the center of the pot is slightly elevated and the seedlings on the outside are planted with a slight tilt.

Basics 4: Techniques to achieve balance when there are few seedlings

Utilizing space well and creatively filling in gaps results in a beautiful arrangement.

Contrast and spacial balance are key.

For arrangements that emphasize the vast space within the pot, emphasizing each succulent enhances their beauty. For diorama-like arrangements, consider each succulent as a piece of the landscape. In both styles, start by positioning the largest or main plant, followed by the supporting ones. Adding small items or accessories greatly enhances the overall look.

Type A: Create a space between plants and arrange them well.

Group planting with only Sempervivum species to create a sense of unity.

I've gathered only plants from the Sempervivum genus to create an arrangement with a sense of unity. Creating several spaces within the container allows you to emphasize each plant and makes it easier to achieve balance.

Type B: Sporadically positioning the plants

By scattering seedlings across a large space, I create a landscape reminiscent of an African safari. To depict the vast plains, I planted seedlings of similar (low) height.

Basics 5: Filling in gaps to achieve balance

Complete a round bouquet-like finish for a beautiful and vibrant look.

Create an Arrangement Reminiscent of a Flower Bouquet.

Arrangements where spaces between plants are filled up are my specialty. This style is recommended when aiming for a vibrant pot. Succulents can be easily planted if their roots are elongated, allowing for numerous plants in one pot. However, succulents dislike humidity, so be cautious about overcrowding them, especially during the rainy season and summer.

Type A: Planting densely like a bouquet

The basic idea is to create a high rounded center. This will reduce the amount of soil in the pot and allow the seedlings to grow slowly, maintaining that compact shape for a longer time.

Type B: Planting with some gaps

Arrangements with cacti, using large or mutated plants. Incorporating plants like Monstrose Variegata or Cristata in cavities, and adding round Leninghausii and Bocasana for variation.

Plants are not positioned too close to each other, creating some gaps. Using height differences, angles, and variations gives the appearance of a greater multiplicity of plants.

Basics 6: Use hanging and trailing plants for dramatic effect

A style that expresses elegance and femininity

Add movement to create eye-catching works of art

Hanging pots/arrangements are impactful and draw attention. Using plants with trailing stems overflowing from the pot produces a sense of dynamism and elegance. It's also exciting to see how they grow.

Choosing species like Capencis, Rowleyanus, and Tricolor, which have elongated stems. Even dividing the plants and planting them in two or three spots is effective.

How to Maintain a Succulent Container Garden

As time goes by, plants grow and the form of the arrangement changes. Here are ways to create an environment for the healthy growth of succulents and maintenance techniques for post-growth arrangements.

Basics 1: Varying plant location and management by season

Avoid excessive humidity and direct sunlight in summer, and allow sufficient sunlight and ventilation.

Locations for Spring, Summer, and Fall

Manage for beauty and health, being wary of stuffiness and excessive growth.

The appropriate location for succulent arrangements is a place that receives plenty of sunlight and has good ventilation. Poor sunlight and ventilation can lead to undesirable leaf coloration, stretched gaps between leaves, and weakened plants. In spring, grow them outdoors where there's good ventilation and expose them to as much sunlight as possible. A little rain is not a problem, but during heavy rainy periods, manage them under eaves where they can avoid the rain. In midsummer, strong sunlight can cause leaf burn, and too much humidity can lead to rot. Therefore, place them in a semi-shady spot with good ventilation and manage them in a slightly dry condition. In fall, like spring, grow them outdoors with plenty of sunlight.

Detached houses
Place under well-lit eaves to avoid rain exposure. Avoid placing directly on asphalt or concrete, as ground heat will be transmitted to the pot.

Apartment Buildings
As with detached houses, don't place them directly on concrete floors; use a stand.

Near an indoor window
Place them near windows where they receive sufficient sunlight. Ventilation is also necessary, so occasionally circulate the air.

For densely planted groups
When a lot of plants are grouped closely together, rotate the pot from time to time to ensure that all the plants get sufficient sun.

Winter Location

Manage the temperature to prevent succulents from freezing, and keep them slightly dry.

Most succulents are cold-resistant to around 41°F (5°C). Manage them in a location where the nighttime temperature stays above 41°F (5°C), such as under eaves or indoors where they receive sunlight. In colder regions, even indoor windowsills can freeze, so move them away from the windows at night. If temperatures remain above 32°F (0°C), with the exception of particularly cold-sensitive varieties, you can keep them under eaves or on balconies, keeping them slightly dry. Covering them with plastic during the night is also recommended.

Basics 2: Tips for daily care, watering and fertilizing

Succulents, with their water storage capability in leaves, need less frequent watering.

Water and fertilize in moderation and maintain balance between the two

Regarding watering, give generously once the soil is completely dry. From spring to the start of the rainy period and from the end of September, water until it drains from the pot's holes. Restrict watering during the rainy season to mid-September, maintaining a slightly dry condition. In winter, soil takes longer to dry. From December to February, especially, maintain a slightly dry condition and try to prevent soil temperature from dropping. As March comes and temperatures rise, gradually increase watering.

Regarding fertilizer, if the potting soil used during repotting contains leaf mold or manure, that nutrient supply is sufficient. 5-6 months after planting, use fresh potting soil during re-potting.

Watering from spring to fall
The drying rate varies depending on the location, pot material, and root conditions. If the soil is damp, don't water. For arrangements, water at the base of the plants since there's little space between them.

Watering during dormancy
Water to the extent that the soil surface is moist, once every two weeks. If the pot doesn't have holes, a spray bottle makes watering easier. Restricting water might cause wrinkles on the leaves, but increasing water in spring restores them.

Fertilizing
Potting soil based on pumice stone for succulents might not contain leaf mold or manure. If the leaf color isn't vibrant and growth is poor, occasionally apply solid or liquid fertilizer sparingly. Even 5-6 months after planting, if repotting isn't possible, fertilize to replenish nutrients.

Basics 3: Restoring balance to a disordered arrangement

Prune to maintain the fresh shape and ensure air circulation.

Prune once a month to keep the bouquet-like shape.

To keep the arrangement's form, it's necessary to trim the stems that have grown out of shape. By trimming, you can return the arrangement to its beautiful style as when first created. For wreath-style arrangements, balance is lost when the grass becomes too tall, so it's managed by trimming low. Also, for arrangements in baskets with handles, ensure the handle remains visible. Summer varieties ideally should be trimmed once a month from spring to autumn. Especially before the rainy season begins, reduce overlapping stems by trimming from the base to improve ventilation.

Step 1: Replanting and re-trimming

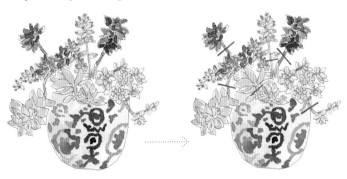

Group planting that has become disorganized
If left for a long time, the stems of the arrangement can grow uncontrollably.

Cut along the red lines
Cut the elongated stems with scissors. Dangling stems should be cut at the base. Let the cut ends dry in the shade for 4–5 days

Remove the remaining seedlings and replant them to complete the process.
As they grow overall, if the pot feels crowded, reduce the number of seedlings and rearrange.

Tips of the cut seedlings

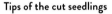

Plant the cut tips and divided seedlings
Use the tips of the cut seedlings and the pulled-out seedlings for a new arrangement. Insert the stems into dry succulent-specific soil and manage them in bright shade for 4–5 days. They'll root in about 10–15 days.

A. Management of summer-growing seedlings
For summer varieties, the ideal times for division, cuttings, and leaf cuttings are from April to June and from late September to October. Plants with many offshoots or those with a lot of roots should be divided and repotted with fresh soil.

B. Management of winter-growing seedlings
Trim during their growth period from October to March. Cuttings are also done during this period. The tip of the stem can be used for cuttings. For varieties like the Green Necklace that have a drooping habit, thin out the stems and cut those that are too long.

Step 2: Points to note when repotting

Repotting should be done at the right time of year. Be careful not to damage the plants and buds.

Arrangements should be dismantled and repotted using new soil once a year. As redoing or repotting can potentially harm the roots, avoid the dormant period. For summer varieties, avoid midsummer and midwinter, and for winter varieties, avoid spring to summer. When doing cuttings, it's vital to ensure the cut end is thoroughly dried before placing it in the soil.

Dividing plants when potting
Separate large seedlings. Hold the roots with both hands and divide slowly and gently.

Inserting the cut-off seedlings
Just as with the stems cut during trimming, insert the stems into dry soil and manage in bright shade for 4–5 days.

Step 3: Enjoy propagating the cut seedlings

Growing baby succulents from leaf and stem cuttings.

In addition to cuttings, leaf cuttings are another way to propagate succulents from stems cut off by pruning. This is a method of propagation in which leaves detached from the stem are placed in the soil during the repotting process and wait for rooting to occur. The leaves must remain at the base of the stem for rooting to take place, so when removing leaves from the stem, do not use scissors. The most easily leaf cuttings are those of Prolifera, Princess Pearl Francesco Baldi, Bronz, and Titubans.

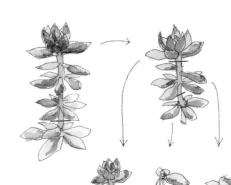

Propagating succulents
Cut stems with scissors and remove lower leaves by hand. The removed bottom leaves are propagated as shown below.

1. Place the leaves the soil.
Place the leaves on top of the soil and keep in light shade. Do not water at this stage.

2. Sprouts appear
Once sprouts emerge from the base of the leaf, move to a sunlit location. Lightly mist with a spray bottle for watering.

3. Roots emerge and the original leaves disappear
In about 2–3 months, once the sprouts grow, transplant to a new pot.

Basics 4: Measures against pests and diseases in succulents
About pests and diseases common to succulents

Succulents are susceptible to pests and diseases, so it is important to create an environment where these are lest likely to occur.
Pests and diseases on succulents are not very common, but high humidity and poor sunlight increase their incidence. Aphids and scale insects are especially likely to occur in poorly ventilated areas, so be careful if you are growing indoors. Occasionally check the undersides of leaves, shoots, and stems. Most pests occur from spring to fall, but some, such as mealybugs, occur year-round.

Aphids
Like general flowers, they appear mainly in spring. They parasitize and suck juices from flowers, new buds, and leaves, causing them to wilt. Control using systemic insecticides. From around February, scatter granules on the topsoil as a preventive measure.

Spider Mites
They appear from around May to October. They're very small and hard to notice. They suck juices from new buds starting from the back of the leaves, causing them to wilt and get damaged. Control using mite-specific insecticides.

Soft rot disease
Occurs during high-temperature rainy seasons when there's a lack of sunlight or excessive moisture. The disease enters through damages on leaves or stems, causing rotting. Quickly remove the rotten parts and disinfect with an antiseptic. Let it dry thoroughly and repot in new soil.

Mealybugs
These bugs have a fuzzy, cottony appearance. They occur in dry soil, sucking juices from roots, weakening the plant. If discovered during repotting, remove the affected roots. Control using systemic insecticides.

Scale insects
Like aphids, they appear on the base of leaves or stems and suck the plant's juices, causing leaves to wilt. Remove them with a cotton swab or toothbrush or control using systemic insecticides.

Basics 5: Q&A about succulent plants arrangements
Answers to general questions about succulents and group planting!

Q. When is the best time to re-trim?
A. From April to June and from September to November, avoiding mid-summer and mid-winter.

Q. The plant is limp and the leaves are wilted.
A. The problem may be root rot caused by overwatering or lack of water. If the soil is moist, it is root rot, so remove the rotten parts and disinfect with a fungicide. After drying the soil well and replanting in new soil, place the plant in a bright shady spot, and after 7 to 10 days, move it to a sunny spot and water it. Wilting of the leaves during the dormant period is not a problem. It will return to normal when watering is increased during the growing season.

Q. Do I need to water the leaves?
A. Basically, leaf watering is not necessary. Leaf watering in hot and humid summer can cause steaming, and leaf watering in winter can harm the plant due to cold. When watering in summer or winter, mist the topsoil and let the roots absorb the water.

Q. White roots have emerged from the stem.
A. When the roots become clogged and the plant ages, it will seek moisture from the air, and roots will emerge from the base of the leaves and stems. Repot and cut back to rejuvenate the plant.

Q. Is air conditioning air okay?
A. It is best to open a window to allow natural air exchange. Avoid keeping the plant in an area where it will be exposed to air conditioning for long periods of time.

Q. The leaves have become sunburned.
A. Exposure to strong summer sunlight or sudden exposure to strong light will cause leaf burn. Move the plant to a semi-shaded area and let it cure. Burned leaves will not return to normal. If necessary, cut them back and wait for new leaves to appear.

Q. The lower leaves have withered.
A. Continuous congestion of roots without repotting leads to the bottom leaves withering. Repot and prune during the growth period and wait for new leaves. Unlike flowers, it's okay to cut without leaving leaves.

Q. I tried leaf cuttings, but they did not sprout.
A. Some types aren't suitable for leaf cuttings or take time to root. Plants in the Sempervivum or Aeonium families, for example, are better propagated through divison or stem cutting.

Q. Is it OK to water the plants indoors the same as outside?
A. Basically, yes. . Water according to soil dryness. Since indoor areas don't have as good ventilation as outdoors, soil indoors might not dry as quickly. Observe the soil's surface and water accordingly.

Index of Plants

"Books to Span the East and West"

Tuttle Publishing was founded in 1832 in the small New England town of Rutland, Vermont [USA]. Our core values remain as strong today as they were then—to publish best-in-class books which bring people together one page at a time. In 1948, we established a publishing outpost in Japan—and Tuttle is now a leader in publishing English-language books about the arts, languages and cultures of Asia. The world has become a much smaller place today and Asia's economic and cultural influence has grown. Yet the need for meaningful dialogue and information about this diverse region has never been greater. Over the past seven decades, Tuttle has published thousands of books on subjects ranging from martial arts and paper crafts to language learning and literature—and our talented authors, illustrators, designers and photographers have won many prestigious awards. We welcome you to explore the wealth of information available on Asia at **www.tuttlepublishing.com**.

Published by Tuttle Publishing, an imprint of Periplus Editions (HK) Ltd.
www.tuttlepublishing.com

12-KAGETSU NO TANIKU SHOKUBUTSU YOSEUE RECIPE
©2013 Kentaro Kuroda
©2013 GRAPHIC-SHA PUBLISHING CO., LTD
This book was first designed and published in Japan in 2013 by Graphic-sha Publishing Co., Ltd.
This English edition was published in 2024 by TUTTLE Publishing Periplus Editions (Hk) Limited
English translation rights arranged with GRAPHIC-SHA PUBLISHING CO., LTD through Japan UNI Agency, Inc., Tokyo

Original edition creative staff:
Original Design and layout: Kaori Shirohata
Photography & Text: Chiaki Hirasawa
Styling: Natsumi Asamiya
Illustration: Juriko Uesaka
Japanese edition editor: Harumi Shinoya
Foreign edition Production and management:
Takako Motoki, Yuki Yamaguchi (Graphic-sha Publishing Co., Ltd.)
Cooperation with Photography
BonBoni (bonboni.net) /
DEALERSHIP (www.dealer-ship.com)
BROCANTE (brocante-jp.biz) / icchu (shop.1-chu.com)
senkiya (www.senkiya.com) /
Reve Couture (www.revecouture.com)
Harutei Unoka
Special thanks: Flora Kuroda Engei

English Translation© 2024 by Periplus Editions (HK) Ltd.
Translated from Japanese by HL Partners LLC

ISBN: 978-0-8048-5610-2

Distributed by

North America, Latin America & Europe
Tuttle Publishing
364 Innovation Drive
North Clarendon, VT 05759-9436 U.S.A.
Tel: 1 (802) 773-8930
Fax: 1 (802) 773-6993
info@tuttlepublishing.com
www.tuttlepublishing.com

Japan
Tuttle Publishing
Yaekari Building 3rd Floor
5-4-12 Osaki
Shinagawa-ku
Tokyo 141-0032
Tel: (81) 3 5437-0171
Fax: (81) 3 5437-0755
sales@tuttle.co.jp
www.tuttle.co.jp

Asia Pacific
Berkeley Books Pte. Ltd.
3 Kallang Sector #04-01
Singapore 349278
Tel: (65) 6741 2178
Fax: (65) 6741 2179
inquiries@periplus.com.sg
www.tuttlepublishing.com

26 25 24 23   10 9 8 7 6 5 4 3 2 1
Printed in China   2311EP